The Impact of Watching Violent Television Programs on Secondary School Children in Tanzania

The Impact of Watching Violent Television Programs on Secondary School Children in Tanzania

Watson Lupogo Masiba

FOREWORD BY
Newton M. Kyando

Mbeya, Tanzania
November 2015

RESOURCE *Publications* • Eugene, Oregon

THE IMPACT OF WATCHING VIOLENT TELEVISION PROGRAMS ON SECONDARY SCHOOL CHILDREN IN TANZANIA

Copyright © 2016 Watson Lupogo Masiba. All rights reserved. Except for brief quotations in critical publications or reviews, no part of this book may be reproduced in any manner without prior written permission from the publisher. Write: Permissions, Wipf and Stock Publishers, 199 W. 8th Ave., Suite 3, Eugene, OR 97401.

Resource Publications
An Imprint of Wipf and Stock Publishers
199 W. 8th Ave., Suite 3
Eugene, OR 97401

www.wipfandstock.com

PAPERBACK ISBN: 978-1-4982-8627-5
HARDCOVER ISBN: 978-1-4982-8629-9
EBOOK ISBN: 978-1-4982-8628-2

Manufactured in the U.S.A.

To my beloved wife Mary and my three children, Theresia, Mpoki, and Elizabeth for their support, patience, and encouragements in the whole process of writing this book.

Contents

List of Tables | ix
List of Figures | x
Foreword by Newton M. Kyando | xi
Acknowledgments | xv
List of Abbreviations | xvii

1 Introduction: The Problem and its Context | 1
2 Television Violence Watching and Related Literatures | 26
3 Methodological Perspectives | 47
4 Hearing Research Data | 68
5 Concluding Remarks | 99

Bibliography | 113

Tables

Table 4.1 Children's Responses on their Accessibility to the Television (N=240) | 69

Table 4.2 Children's Responses on Identifying Violent TV Programs with Acts (N=240) | 72

Table 4.3 Amount of Time Students Spent on Watching Violent TV Programs per Day (N=240) | 76

Table 4.4 Children's Responses on Ways through which Watching Violent TV Programs Affect their Academic Performance (N=240) | 78

Table 4.5 Impact of Watching Violent TV Programs to the Academic Performance of the Secondary School Children (N=240) | 81

Table 4.6 The Relationship between Children's Grade Scores and the Time Spent on Watching Violent TV Programs (N=240) | 83

Table 4.7 Children's Responses on Identifying the Impacts of Watching Violent TV Programs on their Discipline (N=240) | 87

Table 4.8 Children's Frequency of Disciplinary Problems Reported with Action Taken by School Authorities | 90

Table 4.9 Children's Responses on Parents' Role in Addressing the Impact of Watching Violent TV Programs (N=240) | 92

Table 4.10 Parents' Appropriate TV Programs Chosen for their Children | 94

Figures

Figure 1.1 A Modified conceptual Model based on Bandura's Social Learning Theory | 12

Figure 3.1 Map of Mbeya City Council showing the Study Area | 51

Foreword

WATCHING TELEVISION IS ENJOYABLE and refreshing. It has been a customary exercise for youth and adults to watch television at homes and in public places. Some of the reasons that make television watching important are the following: first, it unites people of the world into one community. Second, it is one of the sources of information worldwide. Third, it is the major source of disseminating cultural values of different people. Therefore, television watching is an agent of globalization. However, watching television programs has its own challenges, especially violent TV programs. This means that watching violent TV programs displays bad cultural values of one place and may be transferred and adopted by people of other places knowingly or unknowingly.

The author of this book indicates a discussion on the various effects of violent TV watching in America and Europe. According to the author of this book, researchers on the effects of watching violent media, such as Bushman and Anderson, have the view that "television violence increases aggression of viewers and leads them to behave aggressively in the real world." However, those who oppose (the USA Intertainment Industry authority), "advocate that 'violent media influences behavior in a beneficial way … and TV shows often serve as a release valve for aggression impulses which would otherwise be bottled up, only to explode later.'" To my judgment, the above discussion is important not only to the developed world, but also to the developing countries like Tanzania.

This book is a timely contribution to the ongoing debate on the role that electronic media in general and TV in particular, play to the young generation in schools within the world. While the

Foreword

debate seems to be a common issue in the developed world (North America, Europe and Australia), it is a hot issue in Tanzania as is in many developing countries, mostly in Africa. Television watching has changed social patterns from the households to national levels. This change of patterns has not spared a corner in these developing countries, and Tanzania is not an exception.

The author focuses his research on a small area within Tanzania called Mbeya. Mbeya as an area of focus in the author's study on watching violent television programs provides an interesting flavor. As the author just stated in the methodology chapter of his book, this is because of several reasons: first, the area has a balanced mix of rural and urban setting under one roof making it a better representative of the Tanzanian population for a reliable conclusion. Second, the area is a business center where most kinds of electronic media equipment are sold and bought by different people of the bordering countries (Zambia, Malawi, Democratic Republic of Congo, and Mozambique). Third, the city is populated by public TV halls and show rooms where young people and adults watch various TV programs including violent ones. In this case, the book sheds an important light to the youth not only in Mbeya where the author did his research, but also to the whole Tanzanian country, the above-mentioned bordering countries, and Africa as a whole.

Currently, Tanzania emphasizes on the expansion of public and private sectors to further establish secondary schools for the provision of secondary education. Given the expansion of access to schools with at least one secondary school in each Ward within the country, most of the primary school leavers find themselves joining secondary schools. This excessive joining of primary school leavers into secondary schools makes secondary schools in Tanzania the second biggest portion of the country's social groups. The proportion is even bigger when parents and teachers are included as members of the social groups who select to watch either violent or non-violent TV programs. Hence, the argument of the book touches an important group as far as the work force of the country and the world is concerned.

Foreword

The argument of the author is clear and well-presented. The first chapter is about the setting in which he provides the background and context, the research problem, purpose, objectives and significance, theoretical framework, and the synopsis of the book. The second chapter discusses the various approaches done by other researchers on the subject. The third chapter spells out the methodological approach for the study. The main methodological approach used by the author is "mixed methods research," which is a combination of qualitative and quantitative approaches. Tools for data collection were interviews, questionnaires, and documentary reviews. Moreover, the author examined the required ethical issues surrounding his research work. Following the background of the study, the review of other researchers' works, and the methodological approach, the analysis, presentation, and discussion of the findings of the book seem to be justifiable, reliable, and replicable.

Concluding the book, the author argues that as most of secondary school children watch violent TV programs at home, spending an average of three hours on week days and seven- and-a half hours on weekends, it affects their academic performances and discipline; the effect makes parents to have a role to limit time spent on TV watching, selecting appropriate TV programs for their children, and providing guidance on educational related programs, which are notably missing. Strictly speaking, the book sets in motion the debate on how useful or dangerous watching violent TV programs to secondary school children can be in Tanzania and other developing countries.

Newton M. Kyando, PhD
Tumaini University Makumira
Mbeya Teaching Center

Acknowledgments

THIS BOOK IS A result of contributions from various sources and inspirations. It is not easy to mention all of them here. However, I would like to express my sincere gratitude to the Almighty God: the Father, the Son, and the Holy Spirit, who gave me strength, capacity, and wisdom to be able to complete this book. I could frequently feel God's presence in assisting me with the willpower and courage to carry on. Therefore, without God I could not manage to complete this work successfully.

I would also like to express my heartfelt thanks to the Lutheran World Federation for the main funding of my research. Moreover, I acknowledge the needed support from the Evangelical Lutheran Church in Tanzania (ELCT) and the ELCT-Konde Diocese from the beginning to the completion of my degree studies at the University of Dar es Salaam.

Specifically, I appreciate the support of my supervisor Dr. Mary Mboya, Senior Lecturer at the University of Dar es Salaam, for her valuable advice and challenges. Her patience, guidance, and encouragements made this study a success. The contribution of Elia Shabani Mligo, Senior Lecturer at Tumaini University Makumira, in correcting language and technical issues made this book a reality. Hence, the LWF funding, ELCT and ELCT-Konde Diocese support, the supervision and the language corrections I received made this academic work fruitful.

This book is a revised version of research report for my Masters degree in Applied Social Psychology. I extend my thankfulness to Lwimiko Sanga and my colleagues in the Masters program for their collaboration and helpful contributions throughout the study

Acknowledgments

period. As a result, their rational and constructive support contributed to the completion of this study.

Furthermore, I would like to express my special thanks to the following: the University of Dar es Salaam for upbringing me in this field of study, and Mbeya Regional Administrative Secretary, the Executive Director of Mbeya City Council and the District Education Officer for granting me permission to conduct research in secondary schools under their supervision.

Last, but not least, the patience of my children and their beloved mother is highly acknowledged.

Abbreviations

AAP	American Academy Pediatrics
AIDS	Acquired Immune Deficiency Syndrome
ATV	Abood Television
BEST	Basic Education Statistics of Tanzania
CMAN	Canadian Media Awareness Network
DTV	Dar es Salaam Television
EATV	East Africa Television
HIV	Human Immunodeficiency Virus
ITV	Independent Television
LDCE	*Longman Dictionary of Contemporary English*
MoEVT	Ministry of Education and Vocational Training
NIMH	National Institute of Media Health
NTVS	National Television Violence Study
SPSS	Statistical Package for Social Sciences
TBC	Tanzania Broadcasting Co-operation
TV	Television
URT	United Republic of Tanzania
WHO	World Health Organization

CHAPTER 1

Introduction: The Problem and its Context

Introduction

THIS BOOK IS ABOUT the impact of watching violent television programs to secondary school children in Tanzania. It focuses on the effects which secondary school children get from watching violent television programs under the following subheadings: background to the problem, statement of the problem, purpose of the book, specific objectives, research questions, significance of the book, limitation and delimitation of the book, theoretical framework and operational definitions of the key terms as well as organization and synopsis of the book. I introduce these aspects because they not only set the context of what is going to be covered in this book but also they disclose the rationale and prerequisites of the book. For example, research questions predict the kind of approach and methods of data collection employed to obtain information, as well as the way analysis of data will be done. Furthermore, organization of the book gives the content of this book sequentially, that is, in outline form. Hence, the aspects of this introductory chapter play part as the vital foundation of all material covered in this book.

The Impact of Watching Violent Television Programs

Background to the Problem

Television violence and Global overview

Advancement in technology led to the introduction of television (TV) in 1939 at the New York World's Fair, in United States.[1] Since then, while experiencing its own development and spreading, TV has maintained a stable existence and become an important part of our culture.[2] Today, TV is everywhere and has become a central part of modern life as it often serves as a common thread between people. Hence, without a television means missing worldwide information and not living in a modern world.

During the 1940s, 1950s, and 1960s research began to reassess whether mass media had a great influence on the viewers. The research publications revealed that youngsters would learn behavioral patterns from persuasive media messages which then would be replicated in the immediate future.[3] Another research confirms that more than 3500 research studies except 18 carried out worldwide have examined the association between media violence and youngsters' violent behavior.[4] It also links the exposure to media violence with a number of physical and mental health problems among children and young people such as violent behavior, less sensitive to violence, fear, depression, nightmares, and sleep disturbance.[5] Therefore, the presence of violent programs on television and other media suggests the exact nature of the violence represented and the vulnerable social group of people.

The influence of media violence on teenagers also has been associated with time spent on watching them. Spencer indicates that the American children watch television for an average of three to five hours every day.[6] Another study reveals that American

---

1. Bushman & Anderson, "Media Violence," 477; Nevins, "The Effect of Media Violence" (2004).
2. Rawlings, "Reaching an Agreement," 4.
3. Gunter, *Media Research*, 13.
4. American Academy of Pediatrics, "Media Violence," 1223.
5. Ibid.
6. Spencer, "What do Parents" (2003).

Introduction: The Problem and its Context

children between six to 18 years old will have viewed 16,000 hours of television, and viewed more thousands of movie programs.[7] It is noted that the average child of 18 years old in Britain, Asia, and Australia spent 20 to 25 hours per week as an average rate whereas heavy viewers spend 40 hours per week or more watching television.[8] Moreover, it is estimated that the average American child would have watched 8,000 simulated murders and over 200,000 violent acts on television by the time she/he graduates from high school.[9] In this case, there is a great possibility for secondary school children who spend many hours watching violent television programs to behave antisocially.

The duration of time young people spent on watching media violence was part of their research. Myers confirms that "high exposure to media violence is a major contributing cause of the high rate of violence in modern U.S. society."[10] In addition, Messner points out that constant watching of violent programs has impact on the behavior of children and youths in the United Kingdom.[11] American parents complained that consistent watching of violent television programs influence secondary school children to behave aggressively.[12] It is also argued that watching thousands of acts of cruelty, brutal, boxing match, sexual violence, and extreme violent criminal acts on television leads to distress and pains.[13] In addition, youth who watch violent television programs constantly develop aggressive thought, aggressive behavior and aggressive emotion.[14] A research done in some regions of the world such as Europe, Canada, Asia, Africa and Latin America disclosed that secondary school children and youths who watch violence on television most of their time were attacking others physically and

---

7. Slotsve, Carmen, Sarver, & Villareal-Watkins, "Television Violence," 23.
8. Pretorius, "Violence in South African Children's Television," 2.
9. Gentile, Saleem, & Anderson, "Public Policy," 19.
10. Myer, *Social Psychology*, 377.
11. Messner, "Television Violence" (1986).
12. Christina, Rotzoll, Fackler, McKee, & Woods, *Media Ethics*, (2005).
13. Myers, *Psychology*, 378.
14. Anderson, et al., "The Influence of media," 4.

verbally as a means of solving problems.[15] The same sentiments were observed by other authors who point out that growing up in highly mediated TV violence culture breeds violence in some and desensitization, insecurity, mistrust, and anger in most youngsters.[16] Therefore, constant watching of violent television programs lead children and youths to behave antisocially and this demands adults to protect them from these adverse effects.

Television violence and African overview

In Africa, Television was introduced for the first time in 1943 in South Africa.[17] As a result, there was significant television violence. As a result, TV broadcasting was banned. When television broadcasting was resumed in 1975, television violence was also significant. This marked the increase of homicide rate from 2.5 percent to 5.8 percent per 100,000 in 1987, which was an increase of 130 percent.[18] However, the causes of homicide in South Africa by then were of multifaceted in nature including live violent societal scenes based on political violence and watching of violent television programs merely accelerated the situation.

Pretorius conducted a study on the violence in South African children's television programs, and found that South African Saturday morning television programs have a high violent content. In addition, the study also found that South Africa TV violence caused children to become aggressive, fearful, and less sensitive to real world violence and understand media world as similar to real world.[19] Therefore, the presence of violent television programs in South Africa influenced the viewers to learn aggressive behavior from social media models and then reproduce them in their real world.

15. Groebel, "The UNESCO Global Study on Media," 19.

16. Gerbner, "Reclaim our Cultural Mythology" (1979); Rodman, *Mass Media* (2008).

17. Centerwall, "Exposure to Television" (1992).

18. Ibid.

19. Pretorius, "Violence in South African Children's Television," 4.

Introduction: The Problem and its Context

Television violence and Tanzania overview

In Tanzania, the Government issued notice No. 142 of 1974 in the Government Gazette banning the importation into the country of television sets and computers.[20] Such discouragements delayed the establishment of modern technologies since adoption to technological changes was regarded as luxury that would broaden the gap between affluent and the deprived.[21] For that reason, in Tanzania, the advancement in technology took a very slow pace.

The dissemination of technological advancement during recent decades has made TV a companion of most viewers living in towns. The introduction of TV in Tanzania was the outcome of liberalization policies of economy in 1980s and that of political system in 1990s.[22] The emergence of liberal policies in 1990s led to the establishment of the Independent Television (ITV) and Dar es Salaam Television (DTV) in 1994, becoming the first TV stations in Tanzania Mainland. Abood Television (ATV) was established in 1998. However, the situation was slightly different in Zanzibar where the first TV station was established several years earlier in 1972.[23] Therefore, one of the most significant values of liberal policies was the introduction of TV and computers which contributed to the advancement in technology in Tanzania.

In recent times, many people in major towns own TV sets, and watch every day especially in Dar es Salam.[24] According to Msina, the TV ownership rate in Tanzania rose from 10 percent in 1995 to 75 percent in 2000.[25] This increase in TV ownership was accompanied by TV violence. In Tanzania, the influx of media violence via TV sets in the late 1990s stimulated a formal discussion on the influence brought by violent media on many aspects of life

---

20. Lwoga & Matovelo, "An assessment of the role of TV," 98.
21. Ibid.
22. Mwakalinga, "The Political Economy" (2013).
23. URT, "Tanzania National Website" (2003b).
24. Almasi, "The Effects of Television" (2010).
25. Msina, "Towards Understanding the Impact" (2000).

such as culture, violence, and children's behavior.[26] The number of TV stations increased from three in 1994 to 16 in 2007. Therefore, the introduction of TV in Tanzania was the introduction of the new culture which evoked new discussions because of violent TV content being represented to different people of ages.

Although there has been an increase in TV viewers in Tanzania, it is unfortunate that there is no direct study on the impact of watching violent television programs on behavior of secondary school children that has been conducted in Tanzania. Still, this does not mean that Tanzanians and secondary school children in particular are free from the influence of violent television programs.

Problem, Purpose and Objectives

This section begins by stating the problem underpinning the watching of violent television programs on the behavior of secondary school children. Thereafter, the purpose as well as the objectives of this book will be stated. Television is one of the major sources of information. It is also the most powerful and influential medium of communication worldwide. In TV, there are non-violent and violent programs. Violence in TV programs creates social problems as many children tend to observe, imitate and reproduce violent TV content into the real world such as mass killing, sexual violence, shootings, fighting, suicides, slaps, brutality, murders, verbal abuse and theft. These violent are not accepted and recognized by societies and families.[27]

Secondary school students spend much time watching violent TV programs without examining its impact on their academic performance and discipline in the near future. Given the negative effects of watching violent TV programs such as learning aggressive and antisocial behaviors, laziness, violent crimes, desensitization

---

26. Almasi, "The Effects of Television" (2010).

27. Johnson, Cohen, Kasen, & Brook, "Extensive Television Viewing" (2007).

Introduction: The Problem and its Context

to violence, abusive language, and drug abuse, there has been a need to address this problem to secondary school children.

Although studies show negative effects on watching violent TV programs for youths, however, there is a paucity of studies that have been conducted in Tanzania on the investigation of the impact of watching violent TV programs on the behavior of secondary school children. Hence, this called for the need of such a study. Therefore, this study sought to investigate the impact of watching violent TV programs on the behavior of secondary school children in Tanzania.

The purpose of this book was to investigate the impact of watching violent TV programs on the behavior of secondary school children. The objectives of the book were to:

i. Examine the accessibility of secondary school children to the television.

ii. Ascertain violent TV programs and amount of time children spend on them.

iii. Determine ways through which watching Violent TV programs affect academic performance of the secondary school children.

iv. Find out the impact of watching violent TV programs to the discipline of secondary school children.

v. Examine the role of parents/guardians in addressing the adverse impact of watching violent TV programs on secondary school children.

Study Questions and Significance

This book is guided by one main research question. The question is what are the impacts of watching violent television programs on the behavior of secondary school children? The main research question is automatically followed by specific research questions which are needed to be answered. These are:

i. Where do secondary school children access television?
ii. What violent TV programs do secondary school children like to watch?
iii. How much time do students spend watching violent TV programs?
iv. How does watching violent TV programs affect academic performance of the secondary school children?
v. What are the impacts of watching violent TV programs on the discipline of secondary school children?
vi. What are the roles of parents/guardians in addressing the adverse impacts of watching violent TV programs?

Therefore, specific research questions are important as the research questions were constructed from them in order to collect data from the informants. The study questions reveal the significance of the study specifically to media owners, parents, and as the basis of other coming research studies.

The study findings may help media owners to structure appropriate programs suitable for youths including secondary school children. The structured suitable television programs should aim at enhancing the reasonable academic performance, discipline, and physical skills. These will help to nurture values that are appropriate to society. In this case, media owners have a great role to play in order to save secondary school children and youths at large from watching violent TV programs.

The study findings may also be useful to parents to help them identify inappropriate TV programs and take measures to help their school going children to watch only the programs that are suitable. This means that parents are responsible for choosing suitable television programs for their secondary school children in order to bring them up with good behavior and become functional members of the society. In addition, study findings may also be helpful to parents to be aware of the number of hours and places which are reasonable for their children to watch appropriate television programs. Hence, this might not only enable parents/

guardians to help their secondary school children to have more hours for studying than watching TV but also suggest suitable places which motivate them to watch more valuable than violent television programs.

The study findings may contribute to the existing body of knowledge about the impact of violent TV programs on the behavior of secondary school children. The study findings may further serve as a basis for research to investigate more about the impact of violent TV programs on various education levels. Consequently, the researchers who are interested and going to explore more on passive and the interactive media may use these study findings to carry out their studies.

Operational Definition of Key Terms

In this section only the key terms need to be defined as other terms are easily understood as readers would go throughout the study. These key terms include impact, violence, television program, and secondary school children. These key terms are defined here in order to explain their usage throughout the study. Hence, clarifying the usage of these terms will enable readers to understand the content of this book.

Impact is the central term of this study. It is defined as the marked strong effect or influence, result and consequence that either an event or situation has on something or someone.[28] In this study therefore, the term has a significant value of indicating that watching violent television programs has strong effect on the behavior of secondary school children.

Violence is another central term and it means a "behavior that is intended to hurt someone physically"[29] as well as verbally. Moreover, the term violence is defined as "the intentional use of force or power, threatened or actual, against oneself, another person or against a group or community that either results in or has a

---

28. *Longman Dictionary of Contemporary English*, 812.
29. Ibid., 1840.

high likelihood or resulting in injury, death, psychological harm, or deprivation."[30] In this case, violence is noted as a person's aggressive behavior which deliberately inflicts harm on other people physically or psychologically.

Television refers to a "piece of electronic equipment shaped like a box with a screen, on which you can watch programs."[31] It is on which secondary school children and other people of different ages can either watch non-violent or violent television programs. Therefore, television is an important device which enables people to get global information they like via different programs.

TV program is also an important term to be acquainted with. It refers to something that we watch on television. The TV program can either be non-violent or violent one. Both of them are being watched by people depending on what they like to watch. Television programs with violence are identified as violent TV programs. Hence, violent TV programs may include different kinds of violence and some of them are heavy boxing matches, karate, fistfight, pornography, verbal abuse, and sexual violence to mention a few.

Secondary school children as a term is defined as the pupils who have completed primary education level which lasts for seven years and succeeded to join a secondary education level which lasts for six years, that is, four years for ordinary level and two years for advanced level.[32] However, in this study, secondary school children refers to all students of Form One to Form Four in the Tanzanian formal education system. Hence, in this book mostly, children and students as terms will be referring to the term secondary school children, and if used differently the context of the sentence or phrase will reveal their meaning.

---

30. Mncube, & Harber, "The Dynamics of Violence," 1.
31. *Dictionary of Contemporary English*, 1705.
32. MoEVT, *Basic Education Statistics of Tanzania*, 11.

Introduction: The Problem and its Context

Theoretical Framework

This study was guided by two main theories namely Social Learning Theory (Albert Bandura's theory) and the Cultivation theory (George Gerbner's theory). These theories are used because they reveal how secondary school children get influenced by watching violent television programs. The former theory discloses how secondary school children and other youths learn the behavior of social media models being represented on television and then reproduce them later. The later theory explains how children come to understand and view the world after watching much violence on television. Therefore, these theories are of great importance as they disclose the impact of watching violent television programs on secondary school children and other youths. These theories are explained in a more detail below.

Social Learning Theory

Social Learning Theory is also called observational learning theory. It explicates that people constantly learn by observing and imitating the behaviors of social environmental models whether they are good or bad but they are determined by the occurrences on which they are rewarded, unnoticed, and punished.[33] The basic term of Bandura's social learning theory is modeling. Both media and the social environmental role models are observed by children in their daily lives. Then some or all role models' actions become reproduced later by the children. In his mass media study, Bandura asserts that the influential source of observational learning at every age is the plentiful and diverse figurative modeling offered by passive media including television itself.[34] Therefore, the most important for children and other people to learn any behavior is through observing and imitating what the role models have

---

33. Bandura, *Psychological Modeling*, 46; Rawlings, "Reaching an Agreement," 10.

34. Bandura, *Social Foundations of Thought and Action*, 70.

been doing. Figure 1.1 depicts Bandura's theory on exposure to television violence which leads to learning aggression and violent behaviors.

Figure 1.1: A modified conceptual model based on Bandura's (2002) Social Learning Theory.

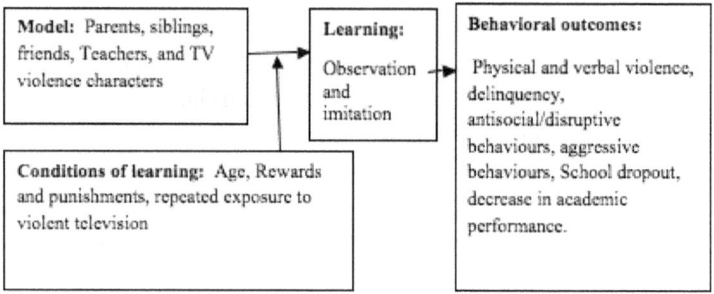

Models in television violence are violent characters whose images are represented on television whereas social environmental models include parents, siblings, friends or peers, and teachers. The violent television models display aggression and violent behaviors which are observed by people with different ages who obviously can reproduce them in future. In a normal circumstance, it is obvious that children are likely to imitate violent behaviors of social environmental models. In this case, secondary school children can also imitate violent behaviors of social media models and then replicate into their real world provided that they are not ignored and punished.

Conditions of learning determine whether learning is to take place or not through observation and imitation. Age of imitators determine their learning and outcomes of what they are learning. Children under 18 and young adults are more vulnerable than the older ones. Rawlings argues that problems arise with watching violent TV programs because children's cognitive development is immature for them to critically understand, organize and analyze

Introduction: The Problem and its Context

program messages if they are socially good or not.[35] In addition, most of the secondary school children watch adult's violent television programs in absence of adults who can assist them to have proper emotional reactions to media messages.[36] As a result, they are easily influenced by aggression and violent behavior exhibited by aggressive social media characters.

Rewards and punishments are conditions of learning by observation and imitation. When aggressive models are given rewards their behaviors will be explicitly learnt and reproduced by the observers.[37] The Social Learning Theory of modeling and reinforcement put forward conditions that influence the likelihood of modeling such as "if the aggressive model is a powerful figure, rewarded than punished for the behavior; if the viewers identify with the model and aggressive behavior is perceived as real and arouse viewers psychologically."[38] Therefore, these conditions reveal that secondary school children are likely to replicate the behavior of the powerful television models who are rewarded and whose behavior or actions are perceived as real and stimulate them psychologically.

Exposure to television violence: Children's regular observation of aggression and violent behaviors performed by television models lead children to copy both exact behaviors that are consistent, unaware and short lived, and the complex social or behavioral scripts that are long-lasting.[39] When aggression and violent behavior of the media models are being watched, imitated, and rewarded consistently, secondary school children in particular develop habitual modes of behavior which may lead them to solve problems violently in future.[40] So, constant watching of violent behavior on television should increase the likelihood that secondary school

35. Rawlings, "Reaching an Agreement," 3.
36. Potter, *Media Literacy*, 58.
37. Omari, *Educational Psychology*, 118.
38. Bandura, *Self-efficacy*, (1977); Mncube &Harber, "The Dynamics of Violence,"8.
39. Huesman & Taylor, "The Role of Media Violence," 403.
40. Anderson, et al., "The influence of media" (2003).

children will include aggressive behaviors into their mind provided that their replication of such behaviors is followed by rewards.

Behavioral outcomes: these refer to behaviors reproduced by imitators, the students. These behaviors might be reproduced by secondary school children; they include physical and verbal violence, antisocial and aggressive behaviors. These behaviors may lead to school dropout, expulsion from school and even jailed. Therefore, these behavioral outcomes are likely to be part of the impact of watching violent TV programs to children and secondary school children in particular.

Social learning theory is limited in some ways, for example, in our everyday lives not all children and youths who watch violent media will imitate the aggressive behavior of the social media models. Anderson and others support this argument by pointing out that not all youths who constantly watch violent media would go out to replicate the observed behavior in the real world.[41] This reveals that besides the conditions that influence the likelihood of modeling, yet the observer has decision to select some of the observed behaviors to model depending on how and to what extent he/she is influenced and perceived them as real and beneficial. They continue arguing that:

> Observational learning and imitation are often thought to be of conscious processes while some types of imitative behaviors are very automatic and unconscious. Similarly, observational learning of complex scripts and schemas such as beliefs, attitudes, and other types of knowledge that guide perception, interpretation and understanding can also occur outside of awareness, even with immediate imitation of behaviors.[42]

Therefore, social learning theory did not consider some of the youths who can only watch violent behavior exhibited on media and cannot replicate them in their real world, and that the imitation of complex scripts and schemas can both occur either deliberately or involuntarily.

41. Ibid., 24.
42. Ibid.

INTRODUCTION: THE PROBLEM AND ITS CONTEXT

Cultivation Theory

Cultivation Theory was established in 1967 by George Gerbner as one of the three cultural indicators project and it aimed at identifying and finding out the cultivation effects of violent TV programs on the attitudes and behaviors of the viewers.[43] The cultural indicators include institutional process analysis, message system analysis, and the cultivation analysis. Researchers involved in each of the three cultural indicators have a particular concern: Researchers of the former cultural indicator penetrate behind the scenes of media organizations in an effort to understand what policies or practices might be lurking there; researchers' concern of the message system analysis was to track the most stable and recurrent images and find out reasons why media produce the messages they do; and the cultivation analysis study deals with how TV content might affect the viewers who spend lots of time glued to the tube.[44] Cultivation theory originates from cultivation analysis research study. This theory states that "the more time people spend living in the television world, the more likely they are to believe social reality portrayed on TV."[45] In other way, Rodman affirms that cultivation theory explains "how people's perceptions of the world are shaped and sometimes distorted by media, and it also predict that, over time, media use will cultivate within users of a particular view of the world."[46] This theory reveals that people who watch television and other media most of their time in their life their way of thinking and understanding the real world becomes altered. Therefore, cultivation theory intended to elucidate that watching of violent TV programs extensively might alter the attitudes and behaviors of the viewers who then can equate the world of TV to the real world.

The amount of time spent on watching violence on television become a significant issue to explain the cultivation effect. Cultivation is a method for judging the impact of television viewing

---

43. Miller, *Communication Theory* (2005).
44. Griffin, *A First Look at Gerbner's Cultivation Theory*, 366.
45. Cohen, & Weimann, "Cultivation Revisited," 99.
46. Rodman, *Mass Media*, 53.

on beliefs, behaviors, and attitudes.[47] Cohen and Weimann confirm that cultivation theory hypothesized that "cultivation effect occurs only after long-term, cumulative exposure to television."[48] Cultivation theory unfolds that only people who regularly watch violence on television become vulnerable to the cultivation effect. This paves a way to seek the amount of time spent on watching TV programs that might have impact on their belief, behaviors and attitudes. Hughes asserts that Gerbner and others categorized three groups of TV viewers, the light viewers spent from zero to two hours, the medium viewers spent three hours whereas the heavy viewers spent four or more hours a day watching television.[49] Griffin confirms that most of the TV programs are violent as a result heavy viewers develop an amplified belief in a mean and frightening globe.[50] This means that their understanding about the social world is altered and they view it as unsafe as television world, and therefore, the more time viewers watch violent TV programs the more they are likely to understand that TV world is similar to the social world.

Heavy viewers of violent TV programs develop different beliefs. At first, they believe that violent TV world is similar to the real world as a result they develop fear of becoming the victim of a crime.[51] This suggests that heavy viewers of violent TV programs would be less likely to calm the worst fighting situation of either between two people or groups of people because they are afraid of becoming part of violent incidents. Another belief is that heavy viewers develop "general mistrust of people as they believe that most people are just looking out for themselves, and hold fast that in dealing with other people, you can't be careful, and do unto others before they do unto you. This mindset is what Griffin calls the mean world syndrome."[52] Moreover, heavy television viewers

47. Shanahan, "Television and Authoritarianism," 438-495.
48. Cohen, & Weimann, "Cultivation Revisited," 99.
49. Hughes, "The Fruits of Cultivation Analysis," 295.
50. Griffin, *A First Look at Gerbner's Cultivation Theory*, 366.
51. Ibid., 373.
52. Ibid.

Introduction: The Problem and its Context

are likely to estimate a larger percent of the community members to be involved in law enforcement and their video world is full of the police, judges and government representatives.[53] Therefore, heavy television viewers perceive social world as dangerous as the television world, and they become numbed to violent incidents happening in their daily lives and at the same time would respond aggressively against their opponents.

Watching of violent TV programs and channels also has similar effects to secondary school children. Those who spend many hours each day watching violent TV programs are also exposed to such a "heavy barrage of violence and crime related imagery, and they come to view the world as more violent and dominated by criminal concerns than it really is."[54] This phenomenon is supported by other studies which showed significant relationship between the amount of exposure to TV and viewers' specific attitudes, perceptions and beliefs about the social world that are derived from TV contents.[55] That is to say, that the actual world is as dangerous as the perceived television world. Secondary school heavy viewers would also become vulnerable to primary effects of television violence. Therefore, secondary school children who constantly watch violent TV programs would also understand television world as similar to real world and that, they would become less sensitive to the societal violent acts as well as behaving aggressively as a means of solving problems at hand.

Besides the usefulness of the Gerbner's Cultivation Theory, yet it has some weaknesses. It does not explain the process how and when the TV contents cultivate heavy viewers' attitudes, perceptions and beliefs about the social world, and it also pays no attention on the interplay of other factors namely individual differences, social categories, ignorance, phobias, biases, and upbringing.[56] That's why, the combination of interacting factors and the

---

53. Ibid.
54. Hughes, "The Fruits of Cultivation Analysis," 287.
55. Griffin, *A First Look at Gerbner's Cultivation Theory* (2012); Oketunmbi, "Cultivation Theory" (2014).
56. Oketunmbi, "Cultivation Theory," 11.

regular exposure to violence on TV influence viewers' perception of the social world.

In this study, cultivation theory is employed to examine long-term effects encountered by the secondary school children who spend many hours watching violent programs on television. The secondary school children who were identified as heavy television viewers were assumed to be altered their perceptions concerning of what the world really is. Moreover, this long-term effect resulting from spending many hours watching violent programs on television is also assumed to affect the children's school academic performance and discipline on the other hand. Therefore, cultivation theory was also found useful to reveal the impacts of watching violent TV programs on the behavior of secondary school children.

Limitations and Delimitations of the Study

The researcher experienced some limitations when he was conducting the study. Limitations are those "conditions beyond the control of researcher that may place restrictions on the conclusions of the study and applications to other situations."[57] Kumar defines limitations as the structural problems concerning methodological aspects of the study, for instance, research design, sampling and measurement procedures, and so on.[58] Limitations were encountered in the field work when the researcher was using instruments for data collection. For example, during one to one interview with teachers, few teachers had little co-operation and the reason given was that they were busy teaching. However, the researcher managed to obtain the required data by making other appointment dates with them. Again, some parents were coming late to the focus group discussions sessions as they had different timetable according to their different occupations. This problem was overcome by being patient and communicating with parents

---

57. Best, & Khan, *Research in Education*, 40.
58. Kumar, *Research Methodology*, 203.

Introduction: The Problem and its Context

before the date of FGD sessions. The heads of schools were also very helpful to remind the parents about the appointment dates and time of the FGDS. Consequently, researcher's flexibility on the appointments dates, tolerance and frequent communication with informants made the field work successful.

This study also has delimitations. Delimitation means "the drawing of boundaries around a study, and showing clearly what is and is not included."[59] This study focused on the impact of watching violent TV programs on the behavior of secondary school children of Tanzania, mostly at Mbeya City Council, in Mbeya Region. The informants of this study were Form Two to Form Four pupils in the co-education day schools, secondary school teachers, and parents or guardians of secondary school children in the selected schools in Mbeya City Council. The study confined itself to the impact of watching violent TV programs on the behavior of secondary school children in Mbeya Municipality. Thus, it may be difficult to generalize the findings to all secondary school students' television viewers in Mbeya Region or in Tanzania as a whole. However, since most secondary schools in Tanzania contain pupils from other regions of the country, the study at Mbeya City can still be a good representative of other pupils in the country.

Organization and Synopsis

This book is organized into five chapters. The first chapter presents the introduction and background to the problem whereas the second chapter focuses on the literature review. In this literature review, the chapter surveys both primary and the secondary source literature. The primary source literatures are reported by the individual(s) who truly carried out the research or who created the ideas.[60] For instance, research articles published by educational journals were surveyed. The rationale for surveying primary sources is that they "present literature in the original state and present

---

59. Punch, *Introduction to Social Research*, 267.
60. Creswell, *Educational Research*, 83.

viewpoint of the original author. Primary sources also provide the details of original research better than do secondary sources."[61] Secondary source literature is the literature that reviews primary sources, and includes books, select journals/review of educational research and other documents. Secondary source literature were surveyed since are useful to investigate and find out the variety of materials on a topic.[62] However, the two source literatures are helpful as they express the earlier and existing state of the information on the impacts of watching violent TV programs on the secondary school children.

Globally, most of the reviewed literatures on media violence including television violence come from the Western scholars, and they include meta-analysis studies, journal articles, individual and group research articles, and chapters in books. Some of the reviewed literatures come from the Eastern and Australian scholars. In Africa, few unpublished dissertations and theses concerning television violence on children were surveyed and most of these few were written in South Africa. In Tanzania, only very few unpublished dissertations about television in general were surveyed and none concentrated on the impact of watching violent television programs on the school going children. As a result, the inadequate literature in Tanzania on the impact of watching violent television programs led the author to conduct this study.

Reviewing the literature is important as it informs what kind of information this book has to contribute to the existing literature.[63] In the similar vein, Punch asserts that literature review "indicates gaps in the knowledge in the area, and show how this study will contribute to filling those gaps."[64] Furthermore, literature review is helpful as it guides not only to define the statement of the problem and identify the significance of the study but also it proposes the promising data-gathering instruments, proper study

61. Ibid.
62. Ibid., 84.
63. Ibid., 80.
64. Punch, *Introduction to Social Research*, 267.

Introduction: The Problem and its Context

design and sources of data for this study.[65] Hence, apart from the importance of literature review given earlier it is also useful as it sets the context of the study.

The third chapter is concerned with research methodology. In the research methodology, the task was to carefully identify, describe and justify the methods employed in carrying out this study. Research methodology is an engine of the study since "the construction of a research instrument is the most important aspect of any research endeavor as it determines the nature and quality of information, and this is the input of the study and the output is entirely depend on it."[66] That is why, the research instruments are constructed in the light of and linked to the objectives of the study.

The study used a mixed methods research, that is, a combination of quantitative and qualitative research approaches. Explanatory sequential design was employed as one of the mixed methods research designs. This design guided the researcher to collect quantitative empirical data first by questionnaire instrument and then collected qualitative empirical data by one-to-one interview, group interview or focus group discussion and documentary review. After having both data in hand, the first task was to analyze quantitative data by Statistical Package for Social Science (SPSS) version 20 in which descriptive statistics were used to obtain tables of frequency and percentage of sample population. Then qualitative empirical data were analyzed thematically and there were several steps to be followed such as "familiarization with data, generating initial codes from the data, searching themes, reviewing themes, defining and naming themes, and producing the report."[67] Thematic analysis steps are elucidated in detail below.

Familiarization with data becomes the first step of thematic analysis. It involves frequent reading of "the entire data set before coding in order to obtain meanings and patterns."[68] It also engages the researcher in identifying and marking ideas for coding and

---

65. Best & Kahn, *Research in Education*, 41.
66. Kumar, *Research Methodology*, 142.
67. Braun, & Clarke, "Using Thematic Analysis," 16–18.
68. Ibid., 16.

writing down and interpreting spoken data to generate meanings as well as transforming verbal texts into written texts.[69] As the result, familiarization with data is a key step towards knowing what kind of useful data a researcher has in hand and checking the ideal relationship between audio taped information and the written data.

The second step of thematic analysis is the generation of the initial codes from the data. The researcher generated initial codes from the data manually. Coding depended on themes and was more data-driven as all data were identified and organized into their appropriate objectives of this study. In this step, the researcher's role was to "name and categorize phenomena through close examination of data, and thereafter, data are broken down into separate parts, closely examined, compared for similarities and differences, and questions are asked about the phenomena as reflected in the data."[70] Hence, coding is an important part of data analysis since it involves organization and categorization of data in order to relate the concepts in line with the research questions and respective objectives of the study.

The third step is searching for themes which suit nicely with objectives of the study. The researcher's activity here includes the analysis of the "identified different initial codes that form an overarching theme. Different groups of similar codes were written together into separate sheet of papers and then were organized to form different lots of themes."[71] Thereafter, a critical examination of different groups of similar initial codes was done, which led to the identification of main themes and sub-themes. Therefore, this step is useful in the identification of main themes and sub-themes with their relevant information that go well with them.

Having identified the main themes and sub-themes, reviewing themes become the next step. The step involves the enhancement of themes. The researcher's task was to conduct a thorough examination of themes in order to know whether two candidate themes

---

69. Ibid.
70. Babbie, *The Practice of Social Research*, 365.
71. Braun, & Clarke, "Using Thematic Analysis," 19.

may stand alone as themes or form one theme or be broken down into separate themes.[72] This enabled to verify the rationality of the data set within themes, comprehensible and identifiable peculiarities between themes.[73] As the result, the researcher identified the logical coherence between the data set and the main themes and sub-themes which had a precise reflection to the objectives of the study, and the data set which had no relationship with themes were discarded.

The fifth step is defining and naming themes which mean "identifying the essence of what each theme captures."[74] The task here involves the organization of gathered data extracts for every theme into logical and consistent explanation with accompanying story, identification of the story that each theme tells, how the story fit into the broader overall story about data in relative with the research questions or questions, to ensure that there is no too much overlap between themes.[75] Therefore, this step enabled the researcher to identify the real meaning of the main themes and sub-themes and their respective supporting data which bring logical message with the context of the study. It also paves a way for researcher to engage in the last step of thematic analysis.

The last phase of thematic analysis is producing the report, which is the "final analysis and write-up of the report."[76] In this phase, the researcher's role has been articulated below by Braun and Clarke of which the author of this study adhered to. This includes:

> Writing-up the report in skillful manner that convinces the reader of merit and validity of the analysis which provides a concise, coherent, logical, non-repetitive and interesting account of the story the data tell-within and across themes; provides sufficient evidence of the themes with data in order to demonstrate the prevalence of the

---

72. Ibid., 20.
73. Patton, *Qualitative Evaluation* (1990).
74. Braun & Clarke, "Using Thematic Analysis," 22.
75. Ibid.
76. Ibid., 23.

theme, and supporting with vivid examples or the easily identifiable extracts which capture the essence of the points your demonstrating, without unnecessary complexity.[77]

Hence, the last phase of thematic analysis requires researcher to produce the report which is sensible and had a well organized themes with sufficient supporting data within and across themes.

Thematic analysis of the qualitative research was then linked to objectives of the study with the aim of complementing the quantitative research. This means that after the analysis of quantitative data, qualitative analysis of data followed to explain them. Thereafter, a discussion of the findings took a chance.

The fourth chapter is about hearing research data which involves data presentation, analysis and discussion of the findings. This involves the researcher to justify his work with other literature which have close relationship or reveal similar sentiments in some findings. It also invites rational arguments which lead the author of this study to concur or refute other's arguments. Therefore, discussion of the findings is more than having quotations to support research findings. Chapter five presents the summary of the study, conclusions and recommendations. Lists of references and appendices come after chapter five.

Conclusion

This chapter gives the background of this book about the impacts of watching violent TV programs on the behavior of secondary school children. It indicates that watching violent TV content is accompanied with negative effects to the viewers and some of them include aggressive behavior, fear, depression, mean world syndrome. The statement of the problem shows that there is a paucity of literature in Tanzania on the impacts of watching violent TV programs on the behavior of secondary school children. This led to the investigation of the impacts of watching violent TV

77. Ibid.

programs on the behavior of secondary school children. The study findings might be seen of significant value in three areas such as to media owners, parents and to the existing body of knowledge. Two theories were useful to this study. Albert Bandura's Social learning theory explains how secondary school children learn violent behavior through observation and imitation from media models and reproduce them latter in their social environment. George Gerbner's cultivation theory explains the long-term effects of watching violent TV programs. Organization and synopsis of the study highlights what is going to be done in each chapter of this book. Hence, this chapter serves as an opening gate as it highlights the content of the phenomenon being investigated, the impact of watching violent TV programs on the behavior of secondary school children.

CHAPTER 2

Television Violence Watching and Related Literatures

Introduction

THIS CHAPTER REVIEWS THE related literature about the impact of watching violent TV programs to secondary school children. The literature reviewed covered some aspects of the study namely violence in TV programs, accessibility and average time students spend on TV violence, rationale for watching TV violence, the major effects of TV violence watching on students, parents' role on the effects of television violence watching, the effects of television violence in Tanzania, and the knowledge gap. The review of the literature is useful to this study since it "provides the background and context for the research problem."[1] Moreover, it "serves the purpose of providing a need for a study, and demonstrating that other studies have not addressed the same topic in exactly the same way, and it also indicates to audiences that the researcher is knowledgeable about the studies related to a topic."[2] Therefore, this chapter is important as it highlights the background and context of the study and provides the link and the gap between the content of other literatures and that of the study.

---

1. Creswell, *Educational Research*, 105.
2. Ibid.

Violence in Television Programs

This section intends to unfold television programs which are violent. Anderson and others conducted a review study in America on 'the influence of media violence on youth' and they found that a non-interactive visual medium, television as one of the media has violent programs such as drama, movie, music, and news. These programs as well as video game (interactive medium) influence youth to behave aggressively in the immediate and long-term effect.[3] The outcome of this study is useful since the identified violent TV programs were employed in this study to examine whether Tanzanian secondary school children and their parents also identify them as violent ones. This review study reviewed cross-sectional, correlation, experimental, longitudinal surveys, and meta-analyses studies and came up with what these studies have found in order to justify that frequent representation of media violence have adverse effects unto youth. This is a big different from this book because it is a research based study, that is, secondary school children themselves through questionnaire identified violent TV programs each with the violent acts represented on them. Another review study conducted by Huesmann and Taylor in United States on 'the role of media violence in violent behavior' found that "TV news violence contributes to increased violence in form of imitative suicides and acts of aggression."[4] This discloses that apart from positive information people get from TV news program, yet, there are negative impacts to the youths, however, in this book television news program was identified as less violent. In addition, parents/guardians found the program appropriate for their children to watch as on it global information are obtained. Therefore, this indicates that television drama, movie, music programs contain violence that might do the secondary school children.

The identification of violent TV programs is done by other researchers. For example, Gentile, Saleem, and Anderson conducted a review study in America on the public policy and effect of media

---

3. Anderson, et al. "The Influence of Media," 81-84.
4. Huesmann, & Taylor, "The Role of Media Violence," 395.

The Impact of Watching Violent Television Programs

violence on children. They found that 61 percent of all programs have a number of violent actions, and the percentage increased to 81 for prime-time program and for Saturday morning programs. Moreover, they identified reality programs as the most violent one as it contains 87 percent of violent crimes.[5] The prime-time and reality programs were not included in the questionnaires as they seem to be new in our context. It is good now to know their violent content in order to save children from viewing them. In the similar way, Pretorius conducted a study in South Africa on 'violence in South African children's television programs' and found that "reality and news programs are not suitable and cause unnecessary fear and that South African Saturday morning television programs have high violent content."[6] The first two programs were not included for the same reason explained above. The good information is that African parents are awakened by the Pretorius' study as well as this book to take measure of rescuing their children from exposing them to such violent TV programs, lest they will become influenced and behave aggressively. Hence, disclosing unfamiliar TV programs puts an emphasis that most of them are violent.

Other studies indicate violence represented on the TV programs in terms of percentage. Rodman's book written in the American context on 'the mass media in a changing world: history industry controversy' explains that most of the TV programs have greater impact to the youth. For instances, TV entertainment program is too violent, and premium cable channels and ShowTime contain 85 percent violence of their programming, basic cable channels contain 59 percent of violence whereas programming on independent stations contain 55 percent of violence, and the Network stations include 44 percent of some violence. Rodman also points out that if violent TV characters are not punished the situation become worse.[7] The amount of violence presented in percentage found in TV programs is still rational; however, Rodman does not indicate how these percentages were obtained. The

---

5. Gentile, Saleem, & Anderson, "Public Policy and the Effects," 18.
6. Pretorius, "Violence in South African," 53.
7. Rodman, *Mass Media*, 309.

difference is that, this study exactly indicates percentages of the secondary school children who identify violent programs, which signify that they watch such programs. Consequently, those who watch TV programs containing a great percentage of violence will be affected much as they have great influence on them.

Greenberg conducted a quantitative study in London on violent TV programs which secondary school children like to watch frequently. The study comprised a sample of 726 students. Students were asked to confirm which programs they frequently watched from a list of 30 shows, which had a total of 18 violent TV programs and 12 non-violent TV programs. He found more choices of violent TV programs than non- violent ones. Moreover, it was found that there was imbalance of the list of violent and non-violent programs. He was claimed to bias.[8] The main point here is that students' choice of many violent TV programs enabled the researcher to know that students watch such programs several time. Hence, it is obvious that students who watch violent TV programs frequently will become easily influenced and start behaving antisocially.

Another study disclosed the amount of violence found on TV programs by comparing children's programs to those of adults. Wilson, Smith, Potter, Kunkel, Linz, Colvin and Donnerstein conducted a study in America on 'violence in children's television programming.' They found children's TV programs contain more violence than those of adults. They also found that more than three fourths of violent in children's programs had some form of humor while only one fourth of programming displayed violence in entertaining situation.[9] What they have disclosed is more likely to be true since children are the most vulnerable to the television and media violence in general. Most of the children are easily influenced since their cognitive abilities have not yet developed enough to the capacity of analyzing and discriminating bad from good media content especially when they are interested in them. Therefore, the secondary school children are more likely to be much influenced by violent TV programs than adults.

8. Greenberg, "British Children and Televised Violence" (1975).
9. Wilson, et al., "Violence in Children's Programming" (2002).

In Tanzania, there has been hardly any study that has been conducted to identify violent TV programs which have great impact on secondary school children. Therefore, it is a task of this study to identify violent TV programs which affect Tanzanian secondary school children as they spend much time watching them.

Accessibility and Average Time Spent on Viewing Television by Students

The first concern of this section is to disclose the accessibility of TV to secondary school children or students since accessibility is an influencing factor toward using media. The accessibility to TV violence in the home is not at the same level because of the different economic levels in the world regions, continents, countries, and families. The UNESCO global study by Groebel on media violence involved 5000 twelve years old boys and girls found that, nearly 99 percent of the European and Canadian households have televisions, 97 percent of the Latin –American, 92 percent of the Asian and 83 percent of the African households have televisions.[10] Moreover, Myers in his book titled Social Psychology (10th ed.) written in America supports that the developed world continents including Australia, about 99.2 percent households have a TV set.[11] These findings are unquestionable as they indicate the global distribution of television and widen the knowledge of the readers. The findings of this book add inputs about the secondary school children's accessibility to television in Africa and Tanzania in particular. Therefore, the findings reveal that the higher the distribution of TV in the households the higher the dissemination of violence worldwide.

The availability of TV to children was also revealed by other studies. Kaiser Family Foundation conducted a survey study in America on generation M2 media in the lives of eight to 18 year olds and involved 1500 secondary school children. It found that 71

---

10. Groebel, "The UNESCO Global Study on Media," 12.
11. Myers, *Social Psychology*, 374.

percent of children had television in their bedrooms.[12] Having television in bedrooms creates another chance for children to watch TV programs they want when alone, that is to say that children are self-directing on what to watch on TV, which might hurt their school performance to a great extent. This book goes beyond this finding as it exposes other places where secondary school children access violence on television and these places include neighbours' households, public and showrooms. However, secondary school children from the developed regions have higher accessibility to TV than those from the developing regions whose children without TV in their homes go to other places to fulfill their desires.

In the United States, Patterson's book titled 'child development' indicates that secondary school students reported that "they have access to television, radios, compact disc music players, and handled video games in their own bedrooms. Those with bedroom TV sets reported more frequent use of medium and that had greater chance to access TV violence than those with bedroom media free."[13] However, the dissemination of television sets in home settings indicates the presence of violence albeit very few people in Africa particularly in Tanzania, the affluent ones, some of their children might have different media in their bedrooms.

In Tanzania, studies that have dealt with the students' accessibility to TV violence have rarely been conducted. Therefore, this study has aimed at underscoring secondary school children's accessibility to television of which much violence is seen.

Another subsection of this part is an **average** time students spend on watching television. Worldwide, previous researches indicate various average times spent by children on watching TV programs. Chanfreau, Tanner, Callanan, Laing, Amy and Todd conducted a survey study in London on 'the Out of school activities: Understanding who does what.' They found that much time spent on watching TV programs on school days was most common in the self-governing school children of the same age. Their parents confirmed that such children spent three or more

---

12. Kaiser Family Foundation, "Generation M2: Media," 9.
13. Patterson, *Child Development*, 557.

hours watching television and two or more hours on computer or console games on a regular school day.[14] Their work adds new information of time spent by school going children on playing computer games which is not dealt in this book. The difference is that this book concentrated only on a non-interactive visual medium, television and its violent programs. However, the average time spent by students on screen in London is also dealt in this book but in Tanzanian context.

Hassan and Daniyal conducted a study in Bahawalpur City, Pakistani on 'the impact of TV programs and advertisements on school going adolescents.' They found about 69 percent of the adolescent students spend more time on watching TV than any medium. Thirty-nine percent of students were found to watch TV music programs while 41 percent of the adolescent students spent much time on TV drama programs. Furthermore, they also disclosed that about 48 percent of the students use two to three hours daily watching TV programs whereas about 68 percent of the adolescent students use an hour only on advertisements.[15] The information about TV music and drama programs is quite well; however they are not exactly identified whether they are violent or non-violent programs. The research done which made up of this book unfolded such programs as violent ones and how they affect children's school performance and discipline. Morgan also conducted a survey study in Australia on 'the time spent with media to the people of 14 and above years old. This author found that about 43 percent of Australians spend an average time of 21.5 hours per week watching TV, 42 percent of the youth aged 14 to 17 watch TV for an average of 16.8 hours per week, and 36 percent comprised people with 18 to 24 years old watch TV for an average of 17.9 hours per week. To every respective group of age, the remaining percentages were distributed to radio, internet, magazines and Newspapers; however, TV watching dominates the mass of youth people.[16] Hence, these inputs indicate that most of

14. Chanfreau, et al., *The Out of School Activities*, 6.
15. Daniyal, & Hassan, "The Impact of Television Programs," 34.
16. Morgan, "Time Spent with Media," 1–4.

the youth from Pakistan and Australia spent most of their time watching TV programs more than the rest of media.

The rarity of studies that explain about accessibility and an average time spent by secondary school children on television in Africa and Tanzania in particular paved an opportunity for this book to unfold such information. Hence, this will show how many hours secondary school children spend on watching TV programs and how such hours spent affect their school performance and discipline.

Rationale for Watching Television Violence

Watching violence on television has become part and parcel for the viewers of TV programs. Nevins conducted a study in Canada on 'the effects of media violence on secondary school adolescent health.' Nevins found that students like other people watch television violence entertainment in order to "satisfy their need for arousal."[17] This means that watching violent television actors inspires strong emotions in them and increases the chance for them to behave violently or become fearful. Moreover, students are also "fascinated by shameless and unusual violation of social norms in violent TV programs as they see these as larger than life transgressions in everyday experience."[18] The findings of Nevins are significant as they reveal that youths can purposely decide to watch violent TV programs to meet their desired needs while at the same time try to compare the media transgression from that of actual world. As a result, most of the youth become easily influenced by violent television performers especially when they are interested in their actions.

Bushman and Anderson conducted a study on 'media violence and the American Public in United States.' They found that television violence increases aggression of viewers and leads them to behave aggressively in the real world. Their opponent, the

---

17. Nevins, "The Effect of Media Violence," 14.
18. Ibid., 16.

entertainment industry advocates that "violent media influence behavior in a beneficial way... and TV shows often serve as a release valve for aggression impulses which would otherwise be bottled up, only to explode later."[19] When psychologists advocate that watching media violence influence young people to behave violently in their real world and inviting government people to join hand to rescue teenagers, the entertainment industry people found that if they concur with psychologists suggestions they will deprive economically. Therefore, for them the defense mechanism is to resist the truth and continue with their business. Anderson and others found that youth watch violence represented in media since they want to identify with aggressive characters and most of them become attracted by the media models.[20] However, scientific evidence of psychologists maintains that both qualitative and quantitative meta-analyses reviews indicate that viewing TV violence increases aggression of the viewers.[21] A study conducted by Goldstein (1998) in United States on 'the attractions of violent entertainment found that both males and females enjoy TV violence entertainment.' He also found that female students preferred TV programs without violence as compared to males who were fond of watching violent TV programs.[22] Additionally, the social purpose for male students to engage in media violence entertainment was to show their peers that males have an opportunity to demonstrate their mastery of various violent images to the certain members of their society.[23] Consequently, the more they concentrate on violent TV programs the more they become influenced and behave violently in the social world.

Furthermore, Dowing, Mohammadi and Mohammadi in their book entitled 'Questioning the Media: A Critical Introduction' affirm that people watch TV programs with various purposes such as:

19. Bushman, & Anderson, "Media Violence," 479.
20. Anderson, et al. "The influence of media," 81.
21. Ibid., 82–83; Huesmann, & Taylor, "The Role of Media Violence," 397; Gentile, Saleem, & Anderson, "Public Policy and the Effects of Media Violence," 15.
22. Goldstein, *Why we Watch* (1998).
23. Ibid.

> Finding information about the society and world, gaining insight into oneself, integrating within social identity, for personality identity, and for entertainment purposes that is being diverted from problems, relaxation, getting aesthetic pleasure and enjoyment, filling time, emotional release, and sexual arousal.[24]

The information about the rationale for watching television violence becomes an important input for this study since it explains the intention that youths and school going children lead them to watch both non-violent and violent TV programs. However, the information was not part of the research work of this book still was found beneficial to be part of the background of this study

The Major Effects of Television Violence Watching on Students

Aggression is one of the major effects of watching television violence. According to Myers aggression is the physical or verbal behavior intended to harm or hurt someone.[25] A study done by Gentile, Saleem, and Anderson in America on public policy and the effects of media violence on children define aggression as "a behavior that is intended to harm another individual who is motivated to avoid the harm."[26] These researchers appended a very important clause to the former definition 'who is motivated to avoid the harm.' This means that aggression is directed to a thinking being, who feels pain and able to escape and either ready to retaliate verbally or physically. Verbal aggression refers "to saying hurtful things to the targeted person whereas physical aggression range from less serious acts such as shoving, pushing, fighting, to more serious physical assaults and fighting, extending to violent acts that carry a significant risk of serious injury."[27] The definitions

24. Dowing, Mohammadi, & Mohammadi, *Questioning the Media*, 16.

25. Myers, *Social Psychology*, 355.

26. Gentile, Saleem, & Anderson, "Public Policy and the Effects of Media Violence," 16–17.

27. Anderson, et al. "The Influence of Media," 82–83.

exclude all unintentional actions performed by a person to another individual victim. There are two types of aggression namely instrumental aggression and hostile aggression. Instrumental aggression refers to "an aggression that aims to injure as a means to some other end whereas hostile aggression is an aggression driven by anger and performed as an end in it."[28] However, all violent actions learned from watching violent media role models and applied deliberately to other people in the real world is aggression.

International Society for Research on Aggression (ISRA) affirms that "over the past 50 years, a large number of studies conducted around the world have shown that watching violent TV programs, watching violent films, or playing video games increases the likelihood for aggressive behavior."[29] The ISRA provides the evidence that exposure to violent media establishes the likelihood that the children might behave aggressively in actual world. Some of the studies include:

> Experimental studies, with people assigned randomly to be exposed to violent or nonviolent media have demonstrated that violent media can cause increased probability of aggression in short term; many cross-sectional surveys have shown that people who are regular exposed to more violent media have increased the probability of behaving more aggressively in the real life; a small set of longitudinal has shown that children who grow up constantly exposed to violent media have a greater risk of behaving aggressively in real life as adolescents and adults, and the published meta-analyses reveal that exposure to media violence can both increase aggressive behavior in a variety of forms and the aggressive thoughts, aggressive feelings, aggressive physiological arousal and decrease prosocial behavior.[30]

---

28. Myers, *Social Psychology*, 355.

29. International Society for Research on Aggression (ISRA), "Report of the Media," 336.

30. Ibid.

Hence, such studies support that indeed irregular or consistent children's exposure to violent media can establish the greater chance to behave more aggressively in the real world.

Ledingham, Ledingham & Richardson conducted a survey study in Canada on 'the effect of media violence on children between the ages of 12 to 17 years.' They found that children's constant exposure to TV and other media lead them to observe and imitate aggressive behaviors and violent acts. These behaviors are stored in their scripts and memorized as part of their behavior when they need to demonstrate it in order to get what they want.[31] Secondary school children will respond to the aggressive behavior they learned by watching violence, if they believe that the violence is genuine and the TV violence role models are like them. The same sentiment has been expressed by Huesmann's theory of observational learning and behavior scripts that memories of aggressive behavior are stored and later recalled in a similar situation.[32] According to Huesmann daydreaming about aggressive acts strengthens the scripts previously learned that are encoded in memory. Huesmann emphasizes the importance of cues in the environment for the retrieval of particular patterns of aggression behavior.[33] Therefore, watching aggressive media models lead children to learn, store, and memorize scripts of aggressive behaviors and then replicate them later in a similar situation.

A study conducted in America by Bushman and Huesman on the effect of media violence on society gave determinant factors for a script to be retrieved. These are "if the situation is very similar to the one watched in TV programs and the violence is realistic, the script will be retrieved. If the children identify with TV role models and the character receives positive reinforcement or has desirable characteristics, the script will be retrieved."[34] In addition, aggressive scripts will be retrieved when cues in the

---

31. Ledingham, Ledingham, & Richardson, "The Effect of Media Violence" (2003).

32. Huesmann, "Psychological Processes" (1986).

33. Ibid.

34. Bushman & Huesmann, "Effects of Televised Violence," 236–237.

immediate situation play a vital role in script recovery as well as cue-activated thoughts and feelings.[35] Therefore, without these determinant factors secondary school children would fail to retrieve the learned aggressive scripts. This means that media role models were either ignored or boring.

Dubow and Miller conducted a study in America on television violence watching and aggressive behavior. They found that long-term exposure to violent TV programs grants secondary school children with a better chance to create aggressive scripts in their memory, whereas short-term exposure to violent representations activates the previously acquired aggressive scripts and stimulates aggression related thoughts and feelings.[36] These authors suggest that long-term exposure to TV violence can guide to the maintenance of aggressive scripts. Aggressive scripts can also be strengthened by long-term exposure; this in turn guides children in developing general strategies for aggressive behavior besides those already in the memory. They also unfold elements that affect script establishment, maintenance and retrieval. These elements include "situational environmental factors, that is, family TV environment and the presence of other people when viewing the violent display, and the individual characteristics such as emotional, arousal, understanding of the violent display, and attribution about the other person's behavior."[37] Hence, long-term exposure to TV violence, the appropriate situational factors and the individual characteristics will enable the secondary school children to observe and learn well the aggressive behavior exhibited in the violent TV programs, and make easier for them to establish, maintain, and retrieve aggressive scripts.

Desensitization to violence is the second effect of watching media violence. According to Nevins desensitization to violence refers to the reduction of cognitive, emotional, and behavioral responses to real world violence. Moreover, Nevins argues that

---

35. Huesmann, "Psychological Processes" (1986b); Berkowitz, "Situational Influences on Relations" (1986).
36. Dubow & Miller, "Television Violence Viewing," 36.
37. Ibid.

cognitive desensitization lessens people's feelings of concern, empathy, and sympathy toward the victim of the real world violence.[38] Gerbner conducted a study in America on 'reclaim our cultural mythology: television's global marketing strategy creates a damaging and alienated window on the world.' Gerbner found that TV violence desensitizes viewers to suffering and those viewers lose the ability to understand the consequences of real world violence, to empathize, to resist and to protest.[39] His findings are beyond-doubt; however, people who mostly watch real world violence in social gatherings also become desensitized to real life violence since some of them delay to calm the situation and others feel less concerned when others fight in their presence.

Bushman and Anderson conducted an experimental study on 'comfortable numb: desensitizing effects of violent media on helping others.' They conducted two lab experiments. The first one was for violent video games with 320 participants (160 males and 160 females), college students while the second was for violent TV Movie with 162 participants, the adult moviegoers. In the first lab experiment, there was a real fight between two actors and before them there were college students who watched violent video games and those who watched non-violent video games. Bushman and Anderson found that students "who played violent video games took longer time over 450 percent to help the victim than who played nonviolent video games. They also found that violent gamers were less likely to notice the fight and considered it less severe, which are two obstacles to helping"[40] In the second lab experiment, the participants had a chance to help a young lady with enfolded ankle that dropped the crutches outside the movie theatre and struggling to retrieve them. They found that participants who watched violent TV movies took longer time over 26 percent to help the young lady than the participants who watched non-violent TV movies. They also found that women provide less help than men, and that violent media desensitize viewers to the

38. Nevins, "The Effect of Media Violence" (2004).
39. Gerbner, "Reclaim our Cultural Mythology" (1994).
40. Bushman, & Anderson, "Comfortably Numb," 273–276.

pain and sufferings of others. For both studies, they concluded that desensitization caused by violent media generalizes beyond failure to help sufferers of violence.[41] These lab experiment studies' participants were grown up people and become desensitized by media violence. This indicates that desensitization to violence effect goes beyond the boundaries of secondary school people's age. Hence, it is obvious that secondary school children who consistently play video games and watch violent TV movies would also become desensitized to real world violence. These experiments guide to think that desensitization to violence effect would be even high for primary school children.

Many research studies have confirmed for a long time that constant watching of media violence, desensitizes people to the real world violence, and the most dangerous and powerful effect of media violence is to make all of us insensitive to real life violence.[42] Therefore, absolutely regular exposure to violent TV programs and other violent media desensitize people to real-life violence.

Desensitization to real world violence as one of the effects of watching TV violence was not part of the research work belonging to this book. However, African and Tanzanian secondary school children who constantly watch or play media violence and particularly violent TV programs have greater chance to become desensitized to the real world violence just as other school going children and adults found in other global regions.

The third effect of television violence watching on students is a mean world syndrome. Slotsve, Carmen, Sarver, and Watkins conducted a study in United States on 'television violence and aggression: a retrospective study.' They found that watching violent TV programs adds the fear of becoming a victim and a sense of mistrusting other people.[43] The findings of these authors are certain as people who constantly watch violent media content fail to differentiate the world of media from real world. As a result, they

41. Ibid., 276–277.
42. American Academy Pediatrics. "Media Violence," 1223.
43. Slotsve, et al., "Television Violence," 27.

come to understand that real world people are as dangerous as those viewed on violent media.

The same sentiment has been extended by Gerbner, Gross, Signorielli and Morgan who conducted a study in United States on 'television violence, victimization, and power. They also found that people who watch violent TV content extensively do not see the differences between TV world and the real world. Moreover, they see the real world as unsafe and are more worried of walking alone in their own neighbourhoods during the nighttime, and this is known as 'mean world syndrome—a belief that the real world is unsafe place.[44] Therefore, heavy viewers are more likely than light viewers to see the real world as dangerous as the media world.

In addition, Lefkowitz and Huesmann as found in Slotsve and others support that the more people watch violent TV programs the more mistrustful the people are and the greater the people's expectation of being involved in the societal violence.[45] The tendency of watching violent TV programs extensively lead people to be suspicious of others since they're afraid of becoming victims. So, they build a schema of intentional protective measures with an expectation that the real world is full of violence.

The fourth effect of TV violence watching is on academic performance of students. Many studies have revealed that there is a negative relation between regular exposure to media violence and academic performance of the students.[46] Hence, these studies endorse that watching media violence including television violence have serious effect on school performance of the students who watch such media extensively. Longitudinal survey study carried out in United Kingdom by Johnson, Cohen, Kasen, and Brook on 'TV violence viewing in adolescents.' The children were studied five times at the interval of three years. They found that high levels of exposure to television were associated with lower

44. Gerbner, at al., "Television Violence," 710.
45. Slotsve, et al., "Television Violence" (2008).
46. Thompson, & Austin, "Television Viewing and Academic" (2003); Johnson, et al., "Extensive Television Viewing" (2007); Daniyal, & Hassan, "The Impact of Television" (2013).

levels of educational achievement in early adulthood.[47] According to the nature of longitudinal study, the finding is quite fine because it assesses the long term effect of violent media content to the viewers. This means that the effects of violent media become revealed in the students who are fond of watching such type of media. Therefore, the childhood regular exposure to Violent TV programs and other media is related to adolescents and young adults' poor performance.

Another research was conducted in Bahawalpur City, Pakistan by Daniyal and Hassan on 'the impacts of TV programs and advertisements on school going adolescents aged 13-16 years old.' They found that, watching non-violent or violent TV programs prevent students from intellectual thinking, which led the performance and grades of the students to decrease. The findings are unquestionable as authors have an opinion that the amount of time spent on watching whether nonviolent or violent media is the most determining factor on students' academic performance. Moreover, they assert that intellectual thinking capacity decreases since watching the media heroes for a long time does not require high thinking capacity of the viewers, only minimal capacity is required.[48] As a result, the more time spent on watching either nonviolent or violent television the more the poorer students' academic performance since the cognitive higher order for challenging class work become deteriorated.

The amount of time spent on watching television has been extended by Thompson and Austin who conducted a survey study on 'the effect of watching television and advertisements in Pakistan involving all adolescents.' They found that students' performance depend on the amount of time they spend on television content. They also indicated that children who spend more than 10 hours watching TV their class assignments will be done poorly and when the amount of time exceeds 30 hours per week the situation will be even worse.[49] These findings are supported by Almasi

47. Johnson, et al., "Extensive Television Viewing" (2007).
48. Daniyal, & Hassan, "The Impact of Television" (2013).
49. . Thompson, & Austin, "Television Viewing and Academic" (2003).

who conducted a study in Tanzania on 'television viewing habits.' Almasi found that high exposure to TV programs had adverse effects on children's learning such as school dropout and decrease in academic achievement.[50] Therefore, the amount of time spent on watching TV programs has a negative effect on students' performance.

The ways through which TV violence watching affects the performance of secondary school students has not been conducted in Tanzania and in sub-Saharan Africa at large. Therefore, this study has to reveal the ways through which TV violence watching affects academic performance of the students in Tanzania.

Television violence watching also leads students to behave violently. Anderson and his colleagues conducted a longitudinal meta-analysis study on the 'influence of media violence on youth in America.' It involved 5,000 youth participants. They found that extensive watching violent TV programs in childhood promoted aggression in later childhood, adolescents, and in young adults. They also found that youths, who spent more time watching TV violence argued more often with teachers, get into more fights at school, became less sensitive to real life of violence, and saw the world as more hostile.[51] In addition, such students also involve themselves in school shootings and killing themselves, and killing their neighbours, and sometimes their siblings by employing techniques learned from role models of violent TV programs.[52] The findings are unquestionable, and it is obvious to most of the students with high exposure to violent TV programs to behave antisocially. As a result, such secondary school children become hated by other students as well as their teachers. The findings are useful as they open up a discussion to this book on the impact of watching violent TV programs to the discipline of the students which is discussed in detail in chapter four.

50. Almasi, "The Effects of Television Viewing" (2010).
51. Anderson, et al. "The Influence of Media Violence" (2003).
52. Centerwall, "Television and Violence" (1992); Baron, Branscombe, & Byrne, *Social Psychology*, (2009); King, *The Science of Psychology* (2011).

The Impact of Watching Violent Television Programs

Huesman conducted randomized experiments in America on 'exposure of children and youth to violent TV and films.' The purpose of the study was to understand whether children and youth exposure to violent TV and films caused them to behave aggressively. Two groups of youth were selected randomly. Group one was highly exposed to violent TV programs while group two was exposed to non-violent TV programs. Later, the two groups were allowed to interact through playing a game that stimulated conflict. He found that members of group one behaved more aggressively immediately afterwards than members from group two. He also observed that such behaviors were not only exhibited by secondary school youth but also by preschoolers, college students and adults.[53] Therefore, this indicates that replication of the violent behavior learned from the television role models does not exclude the grown up people, however, children are the most vulnerable ones.

The Cross-sectional correlation study also shows consistent and positive association between exposure to TV violence and violent behavior. For example, McIntyre and Teevan conducted a correlation study on the relationship between exposure to TV violence and aggression in Canada involving 2,300 high school students. They found that youth who were fond of watching violent TV programs were more likely to disobey their parents and engage in antisocial/delinquent behavior. The correlations obtained were usually between 0.15 to 0.3 which is between extremely low correlation coefficient and low correlation coefficient.[54] Correlation research does not provide evidence for causal relationship; yet, the behavior is assessed in the natural settings and makes researchers to be more confident that their findings are applicable to general population.[55] Therefore, correlation study reveals that watching violent TV programs creates a behavior gap between school children and their parents/guardians as most of their children prefer what they learnt on violent TV role models to parents' guidance.

---

53. Huesmann, "The Impact of Electronic Media" (2007).
54. McIntyre, and Teevan, *Television and Social Behavior* (1972).
55. Nevins, "The Effect of Media Violence," 14.

Television Violence Watching and Related Literatures

The behavior gap between secondary school children and the parents/guardians become a very important point of discussion in this study. Huesmann and Taylor assert that parents or guardians are very important moderators of the harmful effects of exposure not only to television violence but also to media violence in general on their children.[56] These authors suggest that parents have to guide their children's exposure to media violence and discuss their effects with their children in order to lessen the problem. This means that parents have to take an active mediating approach towards media viewing by their children including "commenting regularly and critically about realism, justification, and other factors that could influence learning, children can less likely become negatively influenced by media content."[57] When parents or guardians discuss the negative effect of media violence or restrict their children to watch violent television and video game content, they can discourage children to watch media violence. This in turn, can help children to grow up with less aggressive attitudes. Therefore, parents or guardians have important role to rescue their children from the short-term and long term effects resulting from watching violence in the media, especially on TV which is found in urban and rural electrified areas. With these findings it is exactly known that most of the parents were and/or are unaware that violent media including television violence have impact to their school going children.

The findings of studies on the major effects of TV violence watching on secondary school children are useful as they play part as the foundation and a vital bridge of this study. However, the research work of this book did not employ laboratory or field experiments, cross-sectional, correlation, and longitudinal and meta-analyses studies; yet, their findings gave vital understanding on how secondary school children get influenced by media violence and television violence in particular.

---

56. Huesmann, & Taylor, "The Role of Media Violence," 407.
57. Ibid.

Knowledge Gap

Most of the reviewed literature come from Western countries and less from African countries, including Tanzania. Western findings cannot be generalized because of different operational context, social-cultural, economic factors, and the historical background. Findings from the reviewed literature it is obvious that limited studies have been conducted in Tanzania on the effect of television violence watching on the secondary school students. Given lack of literature on the TV violence in Tanzania and the concomitant effects of TV violent watching on secondary school students, this necessitated the need for this study.

Conclusion

Chapter two is concerned with literature review. It discloses that most of the TV programs have violent content which affects children's way of behaving in the real world. It also noted that the accessibility of secondary school children to television is higher in developed world regions than developing world regions and those who have high exposure to violent TV content become more affected. The reasons for them to watch TV content are many and some of them include TV unites people globally as it is a powerful medium source of information, watching violent TV programs satisfy their needs for arousal, for emotional release and integrating within the social identity. Moreover, secondary school children who are highly watching violent media including television they are more likely to behave aggressively, become desensitized to the real life violence, perform poorly in academics and their discipline is also poor as they often have hostile interaction with their peers, teachers as well as their parents. The impact of watching violent TV programs invited parents or guardians to play their role to rescue their children from the deleterious effects. However, most of the literatures reviewed come from overseas which created a chance for this study to be conducted in Tanzania, a different context of developing world.

CHAPTER 3

Methodological Perspectives

Introduction

THIS CHAPTER CONCERNS ABOUT research methodology. Research methodology is "a way to systematically solve research problem. It may be understood as the science of studying how research is done scientifically."[1] Following the above definition, this chapter presents and explains the methods that were used in carrying out this study. It is organized into the following subheadings: research approach, research design, area of the study, target population, sample and sampling procedure, instruments for data collection, validity and reliability of the instruments, data analysis procedures, and ethical considerations.

Research Approach and Design

This study employed a mixed methods research, which is a combination of quantitative and qualitative research approaches. Mixed methods research is used because it offers a better comprehension of the research problem and questions than either one method by itself, it enables the researcher to cross-validate and confirm findings of the study, and it also provides the best opportunity to deal with specific sub-facets of the research topic.[2] Quantitative approach was used to collect and present data in the form of num-

---

1. Kothari, *Research Methodology*, 8.
2. Creswell, *Educational Research*, 535.

bers, frequencies, sums, and percentages; quantitative research is based on the measurement of quantity or amount, and it also conveys a sense of solid, objective research.[3] Qualitative research approach was considered the most suitable for being highly exhaustive and reliable in making deep exploration of information from informants.[4] It is also appropriate in studying the informants' attitudes, perceptions and opinions in understanding of behavior.[5] Qualitative approach enabled the researcher to obtain detailed actual word information of the respondents in terms of views and opinions on the impact of watching violent TV programs on secondary school children. It also enabled the researcher to get information about the role of parents or guardians in addressing the impact of watching violent TV programs on their secondary school children. Therefore, employing the two approaches in single study does not only provide a better understanding of research problem and question but also provides stronger results than either one approach by itself.

This study also employed a research design. A research design is "the arrangement of conditions for collection and analysis of data in a manner that aims to combine relevance to the research purpose with economy in procedure."[6] The study used mixed methods design. Creswell defines a mixed methods design as the process for collecting, analyzing and combining quantitative and qualitative data in one study to comprehend a research problem and to answer research questions correctly.[7] This definition fits well the nature of the research approach of this study. This study employed explanatory sequential design, one of the mixed methods research designs. In explanatory design, the great task of researcher is on quantitative data collection and analysis. Qualitative data collection comes later and the data are used to explain

---

3. Kothari, *Research Methodology* (2012).
4. Cohen, Manion, & Marrison, *Research Methods* (2007).
5. Kombo & Tromp, *Proposal and Thesis Writing* (2006).
6. Kumar, *Research Methodology*, 84; Kothari, *Research Methodology*, 31.
7. Creswell, *Educational Research*, 535.

the quantitative results.[8] The underlying principle for employing this design is that "quantitative data and results provide a general picture of the research problem; more analysis, specifically through qualitative data collection is needed to refine, extend, or explain the general picture."[9] Therefore, following the meaning of a mixed methods research, the researcher gathered quantitative data first, which were followed by the qualitative data collection on the impact of watching violent TV programs watching on secondary school students. Then quantitative data were analyzed first whereas qualitative data were analyzed later and served to explain the information obtained through quantitative method.

Description of the Area and Population

Tanzania is a large country with more than twenty regions. It is hardly possible to carry out the research to all regions without being superficial. The researcher decided to focus his area of study in only one region (Mbeya). Mbeya Region is located in the South West Corner of the Southern Highlands of Tanzania. The region is bordered by Tabora Region in the Northwest, Singida Region in the Northeast, Iringa Region in the East, and Rukwa Region in the West. In the South, the region is bordered by the countries of Zambia and Malawi. The region is administratively divided into ten councils namely Mbeya City Council, Mbeya Rural, Ileje, Mbozi, Mbarali, Chunya, Rungwe, Busokelo, Kyela and Momba. This study therefore, was specifically conducted in Mbeya City Council, which is located between latitudes 8° 50' 0" S and 8° 55' 0" S, and it lies between longitudes 33° 25' 0" E and 33° 35' 0" E. So, the area of study is generally located in Southern Highlands of Tanzania.

Mbeya City was selected for a number of reasons. It comprises secondary school students from households with different economic status, that is, from high, middle and low income status.[10]

8. Ibid., 542.
9. Ibid.
10. URT, "Household Budget Survey" (2014).

Students from households with high and middle income status watch TV violence in and out of their homes while those from low income status watch violence on television and other media outside of their homes.[11] Secondly, the survey study showed that Mbeya City council had 71 percent households connected to electricity,[12] which stimulates people to buy TV sets. Thirdly, the City council is a business city, thus most of business people have shops with TV sets, and also it has more people with television sets than any other council in the region. Moreover, trading activities also have been going on between Tanzania, Malawi, Zambia, and Democratic Republic of Congo (DRC). Mbeya region is the main border through which imported and exported goods pass through hence making the city a business centre. This leads to the availability of many media electronic industrial facilities. For these reasons therefore, Mbeya City Council was purposively selected as the area of study and hereunder is the map of Mbeya City Council.

---

11. Anderson, et al. "The Influence of Media Violence" 2003.
12. URT, "Tanzania Strategic Cities" (2010).

Methodological Perspectives

Figure 3.1: Map of Mbeya City Council Showing the Study Area

Source: GIS (Geographical Information Systems),
University of Dar es Salaam, October, 2014

Target Population

The target population or sampling frame refers to the "actual list of sampling units from which the sample is selected."[13] Target population for this study comprised of all students attending secondary schools in Mbeya City Council within Mbeya Region. On the one hand, the target population from which a sample was drawn was 24551 students. On the other hand, parents of secondary school students in Form One to Four and the secondary school teachers

---

13. Creswell, *Educational Research*, 381.

in Mbeya City were involved in the study. So, the target population of this study involves all students in Form one to four, parents or guardians, and secondary school teachers who are employed and work in Mbeya City Council within Mbeya Region.

Sample and Sampling Procedures

The first subsection of this part is a sample to be studied. A sample refers to "a subgroup of the target population that the researcher plans to study for generalizing the target population.[14] Getting an appropriate sample size that will fulfill the requirements of the study is not a one way responsible. Some scholars prefer to use mathematical formulae to other means of getting sample for the study whereas other scholars are not limited to use only mathematical formulae. Denscombe argues that, practically, the difficulty of challenging factors of resources and accuracy means that the decision on the appropriate sample size tends to be based on experience and good judgment rather than relying on strict mathematical formulae.[15] Bartlett, Kotrlik and Higgins developed a table for sample size determination of which this study expected to have a sample size between 83 and 623 respondents for continuous and categorical independent variables.[16] Therefore, basing on Bartlett and others, and Denscombe the sample size of this study was 300 respondents, being the sum of 240 students, 24 teachers, and 36 parents/guardians.

The study also involved six co-education day secondary schools. The schools comprised two central government, two community and two private schools. Students from Form One to Form Four from the selected secondary schools participated in the study. Parents/guardians of secondary school students and teachers comprising six heads of schools, six deputy heads of schools, six academic masters/mistresses and six discipline masters/mistresses

14. Ibid., 142.
15. Denscombe, *The Good Research Guide*, 23.
16. Bartlett, Kotrlik, & Higgins, "Organizational Research" (2001).

Methodological Perspectives

from the selected schools were involved in the study. Therefore, the sample size of this study comprised of students in Form One to Four and their selected teachers from the co-education day secondary schools, and parents and/or guardians whose secondary school children are informants.

This study employed several sampling procedures. Purposive, stratified and simple random sampling techniques were used in selecting the sample of the study. In this study, purposive sampling was used to select area of the study, teachers and the parents/guardians of the secondary school students from Form One to Four. The selection of the sample units were determined by the information rich, accessibility, financial status and time. Mbeya City Council was purposively selected because most of its areas are electrified; most of its residents had access to TV programs. Furthermore, the researcher assumed that the prevalence of many violent crime events happening in Mbeya City was mostly contributed by consistent watching violence on television and other visual media. As a result, Mbeya City Council was purposively selected as the area of study.

The co-education day secondary schools, secondary school teachers from the selected schools, heads and deputy heads, academic and discipline masters/ mistresses were purposively sampled. Co-education day schools were purposively selected in order to capture and generalize the effect of TV violence watching to male and female students. Secondary school teachers from selected schools were purposively selected because of their closeness with students. Heads of schools and second masters/mistresses were purposively sampled because of their closeness to students in matters related to administration, and thus they became part of the key respondents of this study. Academic masters become part of this study since they were mostly concerned with daily academic responsibilities whereas discipline masters/mistresses are very close to the students and deal with all discipline issues. Parents/guardians were selected because are the ones to monitor the watching trend of television at their homes. According to this study therefore, these sample units were purposively selected basing on their responsibilities they have to secondary school children from Form One to Four.

Stratified random sampling was used to obtain co-education day secondary schools which were involved in this study. These schools had three categories/strata namely co-education community day schools, co-education private day schools, and co-education central government day schools. These strata were purposively formed basing on researcher's judgment. The researcher used stratified random sampling to obtain co-education day community and private secondary schools. To get two co-education community secondary schools, the researcher wrote 28 names of co-education community day secondary schools, each on a separate piece of paper which then were folded and mixed up. Thereafter, the researcher picked up two pieces of the folded papers randomly. Two pieces of paper were unfolded and the names found were Uyole and Sinde Secondary Schools. The same process was used to obtain two out of 23 co-education private day secondary schools. Sangu and St. Aggrey Secondary schools were randomly selected among the co-education private schools to participate in the study. Thus, two co-education community secondary schools and two co-education private secondary schools were obtained to take part in the study. Mbeya City Council had only two central government co-education day secondary schools which were automatically involved in the study. These were Mbeya Day and Samora Secondary schools. Therefore, a total of six schools were sampled to participate in the study.

Stratified and simple random samplings were employed to get the sample of secondary schools children who were regularly attending school during the research time and whose age were between 12 and 21 years old. Stratification for students based on grade levels, that is, Form One, Two, Three, and Four; and gender, female and males students. The second procedure was to obtain 10 students per class of whom five were females and the other five were males. Lastly, simple random sampling was employed since students were requested to line-up into lines one for females and another for males. Then students were asked to count from one and two. Those who counted two were gratefully thanked and asked to go back in their respective classes whereas those who counted one were asked to participate in the study and taken to the room where they were requested to fill in the questionnaires. As a result, a total sample of 40 students was obtained from each secondary school, and the sample was made up of 20 females and 20 males. Participants obtained were 120 female and 120 male students from Form One to Four and making a total of 240 secondary school students who participated in the study.

The validity of the sample study was determined by employing probability/ random sampling whereby every member of target population had an equal chance to be included in the sample. Validation of the sample was also determined by the inclusion of multiple sources of informants in the study other than secondary school children alone in each sampling procedure as described above. Simply, triangulation was employed to validate the sample size as the study comprised secondary school children for questionnaires, teachers (heads of schools, deputy heads, academic and discipline mistresses/masters) for one-to-one interviews, and parents/guardians for focus group interviews. The sample size obtained for this study is a true representative sample because the collected and analyzed data and the findings of the sample can be generalized from the sample to the target population and to population as a whole. Therefore, validation of the sample of the study based on the sampling procedure and the inclusion of right multiple sources of informants while how truthiness of representative sample to the target population relied on the generalization of the findings from the sample about the population.

Methods of Data Collection

Four methods were used to collect data in order to answer research questions of this study. Methods were questionnaires, interview, focus group discussion (FGD), and documentary review. Since every method has its strengths and weakness, this study opted for triangulation method which consisted of a complex process of playing each method off against the other so as to maximize validity of field efforts, and leading into minimizing threats to internal and external validity.[17] Hence, the rationale for employing each method of data collection and its respondents is elucidated underneath.

Questionnaires were used as the major primary source of quantitative data. Questionnaires were employed because they supply a substantial amount of research data for a relatively low cost in terms of material, money and time; they supply standardized answers, and they are manageable.[18] Questionnaires were also used because of their effectiveness in keeping respondents concerns, due to their objectivity, and their effectiveness in collecting adequate information from large samples within relatively short time.[19] Another advantage of questionnaires was that they encourage pre-coded responses, thus allow for the speedy collection and analysis of data by the researcher.[20] In this study, structured questionnaire with closed-ended questions were used in collecting information from the secondary school children. As a result, questionnaire method enabled the researcher to collect numerous data with minimal cost.

Questionnaires were administered collectively to the students during regular class hours. Students were assembled in one class at each school at agreed date and time via school administrators. Then questionnaires were distributed to the students for filling in their responses under the supervision of the researcher. The researcher remained in the classroom to make clarifications for respondents as per their requests. The total time spent to complete the questionnaire was between 30 to 45 minutes. Therefore, after the completion of the questionnaires by students, the researcher collected them.

---

17. Creswell, *Educational Research*, 536.
18. Denscombe, *The Good Research Guide* (2004).
19. Kothari, *Research Methodology* (2012); Kumar, *Research Methodology* (2011); Creswell, *Educational Research* (2012).
20. Denscombe, *The Good Research Guide* (2004).

Methodological Perspectives

Five-point likert scale was employed to rate items which secondary school children had responded. Questionnaire rating scale ranged from strongly agrees to strongly disagree. The values were assigned from 1 to 5: strongly agree (1), agree (2), uncertain (3), disagree (4), and strongly disagree (5). Questions which were responded by rating from strongly agree to strongly disagree were those demanding the accessibility of secondary school children to television, identification of violent TV programs school going children like to watch, the impact of watching violent TV programs on the discipline of the students, and parents' role in addressing adverse effect watching violent TV programs on their secondary school children. The ratings were summarized into three categories namely agree, uncertain, and disagree for data analysis. The question which demanded the amount of time students spend on watching violent TV programs per day was responded by students by putting a tick (√) on the choices of average hours given. Questions demanding the ways through which watching violent TV programs affect academic performance of the students and its impact on academic performance of the students were responded by ticking (√) at Yes/No. Therefore, all students' questionnaire responses were entered into the SPSS computer program and converted into categories so as to simplify the process of data analysis.

Interview method was also used to gather information for this study. It is one of the sources of qualitative data. This study employed both structured and unstructured interviews. According to Punch, structured interview consists of planned and standardized questions with pre-coded categories of responses. In this form of interview, all informants get the similar questions in the same order. Moreover, structured interview emphasizes logical rather than emotional responses. On the side of unstructured interview, its questions and their responses are non-standardized, open-ended and provide in-depth information.[21] The reason behind of employing these two forms of interview is that the former provides uniformity of information and ensure comparability, whereas the latter provides high degree of objectivity, probing, and

21. Punch, *Introduction to Social Research* (2011).

clarification.[22] As a result, both were found fitting to the mixed methods research, that is, a combination of quantitative and qualitative approaches.

Furthermore, this study used two forms of interview for collecting qualitative data which are one-to one interview and focus group discussion or interview. One-to-one interview refers to "a data collection process in which the researcher asks questions to and records answers from only one participant in the study at a time."[23] One-to-one interview was employed because it provides in-depth and rich information by probing, it allows greater flexibility as there is an opportunity to restructure questions only, and moreover, it is good for generating information based on respondents' priorities, opinions, and ideas for the researcher to obtain valuable insights based on the in-depth information gathered and the understanding of key respondents.[24] As a result, one-to-one interview does not only enable the researcher to collect profound information, but also identify false information given by respondents.

One-to-one interviews were conducted at the school premises where teachers were easily found. The researcher asked questions and recorded the respondent's replies on an interview schedule. The researcher collected data from four informants from every participating secondary school. Therefore, the researcher obtained insightful and valuable information from 24 teachers from the six participating schools.

One-to-one interview is an efficient method for collecting data despite its expensive nature. By having a good plan and target with whom to have one-to-one interview the problem of expenses was overcome. Hence, through one-to-one interview method, the validity of data was established by direct contact that enables the researcher to check the accuracy and relevance of the data being gathered from the informants.

22. Kumar, *Research Methodology* (2011).
23. Creswell, *Educational Research*, 218.
24. Ibid.

Another form of interview method employed for collecting qualitative data is the focus group discussion (FGD). Creswell defines FGD as the "process of collecting data through interviews with a group of people typically four to six."[25] FGD was used for collecting data from the parents or guardians. The method was employed in this study because it encourages informants to take part in an extensive discussion and allows the researcher to obtain in-depth information in an efficient and timely manner for the topic under investigation.[26] FGD is a resourceful method as it enables the researcher to collect rational and rich data from a large number of people in the same group within short time.

This study had six FGD sessions and each with six parents or guardians of secondary school children from the participating schools, and thus making a total of 36 participants of FGDS. Masadeh argues that there is no rule about the number of FGD sessions and the size of focus group members. However, he suggests that focus group research should comprise a minimum of three groups each with between four to 12 members.[27] Therefore, as there is no binding rule, the researcher has to think wisely on the number of FGD sessions until saturation point is reached whereas for the size of FGD members, manageable size that will give in-depth and rich information is to be considered. This argument guided the researcher of this study to have six sessions each with six participants of FGD.

School premises were used for conducting FGDs with parents or guardians. The premises were accepted by parents through consent forms brought back to the researcher by the secondary school children. School premises were easily accessible, convenient, secured and conducive for conducting focus group sessions. The length of FGD sessions for this study lasted between one to two hours. However, there are other suggestions, for example, from half an hour to two-and-a half hours,[28] and one- and- a half to two

25. Ibid., 218.
26. Sima, "The Challenges in the Provision of Counselling," 112.
27. Masadeh, "Focus Group Discussion" (2012).
28. Stewart, & Shamdasani, *Focus Groups* (1990).

hours[29] per focus group session. Consequently, this indicates that there is no exact length of time per session and seem to depend on the nature of the topic and the size of focus group members.

Prior to the commencement of the actual FGDs, the FGD questions were subject to a pilot with target population who did not participate in the actual focus groups in order to establish validity. Before the actual FGDs began, the researcher recruited a research assistant, a college patron, who operated audiotape recorder and moderated our group discussions. The researcher conducted the focus group sessions and recorded information from the beginning to the end of discussion. Later, the audiotape information and that of the researcher were cross-checked and then transferred to computer. In addition, during the FGD sessions, the researcher used to record the date, time, location, category of respondents, and the length of focus group session. As a result, resourceful qualitative data through FGD sessions were successfully obtained.

One disadvantage was noted. Participants were not randomly sampled and thus findings cannot be generalized to the whole population. Triangulation method was employed to overcome the problem as FGD method is said to work well with other research methods.[30] So, this indicates that FGD findings alone can neither be generalized to the target population nor to the population as whole.

Documentary review method was also useful. It is one of the sources of qualitative data. Documents are secondary data both published and unpublished found in government publications, civil society organizations and personal documents.[31] In this study, documents employed were secondary school official documents particularly students' performance and disciplinary problems. Hence, documentary data were used to supplement the primary data obtained through questionnaires and the interview (focus group discussion, and one-to-one interview).

29. Evmorfopoulou, "Focus Group Methodology" (2007).
30. Masadeh, M.A., "Focus Group Discussion" (2012).
31. Mogalakwe, "The Use of Documentary Research" (2006).

At schools, the researcher collected data from the official school written documents such as students' academic performance records and students' discipline book records and governing school board files which were cross-checked with secondary school children's watching of violent TV programs. The researcher used students' terminal examination results of May, 2014 to identify the number of students who scored A to F grades all together from Form One to Four. So, the intention was to get data that give details of whether watching violent TV programs extensively lead secondary school children to behave antisocially and score below standard in their examinations.

Documentary examination results were analyzed digitally by using SPSS version 20 and then cross tabulated against the amount of hours spent by secondary school children so as to know how much watching violent TV programs affect academic performance of the students. The disciplinary problems found in the black/discipline books were cross-checked with discipline problems caused by watching violent TV programs, and then identified the actions taken by the council of teachers and the governing school boards. Therefore, the findings to be obtained were aimed at revealing the relationship between a certain amounts of time spent on watching violent TV programs and the academic performance of secondary school children.

Validity and Reliability of the Instruments

Starting with validity of the instruments, Kumar defines it as "the ability of an instrument to measure what it is designed to measure."[32] In this study, the quality of findings in qualitative research was established by undergoing several methods. The first method was to establish the logical link between the research objectives and their respective questions, which ensured corrections to be done before administering the instruments. This was done through the discussion by both the researcher and the second eye.

---

32. Kumar, *Research Methodology*, 153.

Thus, the discussion aimed at having appropriate research objectives and research questions that enabled the researcher to gather the required and rational data.

The second method was to spend much time to build an outstanding rapport and trust with informants. The essence of this method was to create a suitable atmosphere during the discussions on the topic under study. This enabled the researcher not only to check misinformation but also to ask as many tricky questions as possible that revealed the most wanted information. Consequently, the method smoothen a means of gathering data from the respondents. The method also enabled to collect appropriate and reasonable data for the topic under study.

The third method was the peer examination of instruments. This was done through the discussion with other researchers in Psychology and Applied Social Psychology in particular. These were fellow researchers who knew something about the research work being done. Their constructive comments were included in the study. As a result, the instruments were appropriately constructed and become useful to collect data from the respondents.

The fourth method was the application of methodological triangulation. Creswell affirms that triangulation provides supporting evidence from different sources of data and methods of collecting data to shed light on the research topic. Since none of the methods of data collection provides 100 percent accurate and valid information.[33] Thus, this study employed questionnaire, interview, FGD and documentary review in order to attain and uphold validity of the study. Not only that but also a combination of quantitative and qualitative approaches aimed to serve the same purpose.

The fifth method, the researcher employed member checking, that is, respondent validation. After conducting one-to-one interview with teachers and FGDs with parents /guardians of secondary school students, at the end, both the researcher and the respondents reviewed the information given in order to judge the accurateness and trustworthiness of the data collected. Therefore,

33. Creswell, *Qualitative Inquiry* (2007).

this method enabled the researcher to make some corrections on the some information.

The sixth method, the researcher allowed an external auditor to examine the precision of the process and the product of the report. The auditor also had to check whether the interpretation of the findings and conclusions are supported by the data. The role of an external auditor was vital as poor interpretation of the findings will lead to either poor conclusions or disqualify the product of the research study. Therefore, to allow external auditors to examine accurateness of the procedure and the product of the report is inevitable.

Lastly, the researcher translated questionnaires constructed in English to Kiswahili for parents and students because they were not of equal level of education. Translation made the informants understand what was written, which in turn led the study to have the desired data. As a result, this method enabled the researcher to collect data from all informants with different levels of education so smoothly, and at last questionnaires were translated back to English for consistency.

Considering reliability of the instruments, Kumar argues that an instrument is reliable only "when a researcher gathers similar set of information more than once, using the same instrument and get the similar results under the same conditions."[34] This means that reliability is the capability of an instrument to produce constant and steady result. In this study, the reliability was arrived and maintained by proper administration of questionnaires, one-to-one interviews and the focus group interviews mostly known as focus group discussions. Thereafter, a pilot study was conducted at Tukuyu Day Secondary School in Rungwe District Council, in Mbeya Region, which involved 40 students being the total of 20 male and 20 female students. As a result, the study helped the researcher to restructure some contents of questionnaires or make necessary changes on the vocabularies in order to get the required information about the impact of watching violent TV programs on secondary school children.

34. Kumar, *Research Methodology*, 156.

Again, the consistency of the questionnaire was determined statistically by computing the Cronbach's alpha reliability coefficient. The results indicated overall reliability coefficient of 0.818 Cronbach's alpha and the internal reliability coefficient of 0.846 Cronbach's alpha. According to McMillan and Schumacher reliabilities above 0.7 Cronbach's alpha are suitable for the study.[35] Therefore, the Cronbach's alpha signified the appropriateness of the questionnaire instruments.

Data Analysis Plan

The analysis of data was conducted both quantitatively and qualitatively. Before coding the collected data, all answered questionnaires were cross checked for errors and then data were classified into meaningful categories that were assigned numerical values to simplify the analysis. Analysis of quantitative raw numeric data was done by means of a computer. The Statistical Package for the Social Sciences (SPSS) version 20 was used. The descriptive statistics were employed to derive tables of frequency and percentage of the sample population, depending on what was needed in the analysis. Qualitative data, that is, data in form of words, were subjected to thematic analysis techniques such as familiarization with data, generating initial codes from the data, searching for themes, reviewing themes, defining and naming themes, and producing the report; and thus, thematic analysis reflects reality, determines prevalence of themes, and maintains flexibility and through these techniques main themes were identified, analyzed, and presented per specific objectives.[36] So, written descriptions and quotations were used to present some feelings, views and respondents' suggestions concerning the impact of watching violent TV programs on secondary school students.

---

35. McMillan, & Schumacher, *Research in Education*, 188.
36. Braun and Clarke, "Using Thematic Analysis" (2006).

Methodological Perspectives

Ethical Considerations

As a research based book, the researcher adhered to necessary ethical considerations with respect to the research while in the field. These include informed consent, voluntary participation and withdrawal, confidentiality and anonymity, and acknowledgement and permission to conduct research. These aspects are explained in more detail below.

With regard to the informed consent, the researcher informed the respondents all the adequate information on the research topic under study. For example, the name of the researcher, the topic to be researched, the purpose of the research and how it was to be conducted, the possible advantages that will emerge from the study and how the results will be used were all known by research participants. Moreover, the researcher informed the respondents' tasks and duration of time to be taken when they participate in the research. Therefore, the consent of all relevant parties such as students, parents of secondary school children, and teachers including discipline and academic mistress/ masters, and heads of schools was obtained.

Besides the informed consent, voluntary participation was highly considered. Kumar points out that it is vital that the consent should also be deliberate and without force of any kind.[37] In this study, respondents were not coerced to participate in any way. Participation was entirely voluntary. Participants were informed that they had freedom to withdraw their participation at any time. Hence, this enabled the respondents to make a reasoned decision on whether to participate in the research or not.

Another ethical issue involved in this study is Confidentiality and anonymity.

King insists that "researchers are responsible for keeping all of the data they gather on individuals completely confidential and, when possible, completely anonymous."[38] In this study respondents were assured of confidentiality and anonymity. They were

---

37. Kumar, *Research Methodology*, 212–213.
38. King, *The Science of Psychology*, 53.

told that information they would give would be kept confidential. Since watching violent TV programs is associated with anti-social behavior and desensitization. The researcher alone had access to respondents' name and data. This was done successfully by collecting data anonymously and reporting only group results. Basing on these expressions therefore, the participated secondary schools were labeled as A, B, C, D, E, and F, and none of the participants' name appeared in this study.

Acknowledgement and permission to conduct research were also considered. Ideas borrowed from other researchers were acknowledged, and data gathered on informants in the field were reported accurately. Permission to conduct research was obtained before collection of data. The research clearance permits were obtained from Vice chancellor (VC) of the Tumaini University Makumira, Mbeya Regional Administrative Secretary who directed the Mbeya District Administrative Secretary to offer a research permit to the researcher. The researcher took the permit with him to the selected heads of schools, where the discussion of the purpose and its specific objectives of the study and other procedures of data collection was done. As a result, permission to conduct research and the acknowledgment of the literature made this book alive.

Conclusion

Research methodology unfolds how research is done scientifically in order to solve the problem earmarked by the topic under study. Mbeya City Council is the area of the study as it consists of many households which are highly electrified and a business City with many television shops and shows. On the process of looking the means of solving the research problem, the research approach employed is the mixed methods research. Explanatory sequential design was employed. Target population comprised 24551 secondary school children on one hand and their parents and teachers on the other hand; hence, from which the 300 informants as sample size of study was drawn for generalization. The sampling procedures were purposive, stratified and simple random sampling whereas the research tool includes questionnaire, interview, FGDs, and documentary review. Validity and reliability of the instruments, data analysis procedures, and ethical considerations were employed in this study. Hence, research methodology as the way to systematically solve the research problem of this study underwent all these procedures scientifically.

CHAPTER 4

Hearing Research Data

Introduction

HEARING RESEARCH DATA IS concerned with presentation and discussion of the findings on the impact of watching violent TV programs to secondary school children in Mbeya City Council, Tanzania in order to understand the research findings. The findings are presented into five main parts and in line with their specific objectives of the study, which were to:

   i. Examine the accessibility of secondary school children to the television.
   ii. Ascertain violent TV programs and the amount of time secondary school children spend on them.
   iii. Determine ways through which watching violent TV programs affects academic performance of secondary school children.
   iv. Find out the impact of watching violent TV programs on the discipline of the secondary school children.
   v. Examine the role of parents/guardians in addressing the impact of watching violent TV programs to secondary school children.

Hence, these objectives have been worked out and are going to be presented and discussed in detail below.

Secondary School Children's Accessibility to the Television

The first objective was to examine children's accessibility to the television. This objective was vital because the researcher wanted to examine places where students access violent TV programs. The findings on the accessibility of the secondary school children to the television were obtained through questionnaires, one-to-one interview, and FGDs. The findings from questionnaires are summarized in Table 4.1.

Table 4.1: Children's Responses on their Accessibility to Television (N=240)

S/N	Items	Agree f	Agree %	Disagree f	Disagree %
1	We have TV set (s) at home	217	90.4	23	9.6
2	I watch TV in our sitting room	217	90.4	23	9.6
3	I watch TV in my bedroom	54	22.4	186	77.5
4	I watch TV at my neighbours' house	132	55	108	45
5	I watch TV in public halls and show rooms	148	61.6	92	38.4

Source: Field Data

Note: TV – Television

Table 4.1 shows that 217 (90.4 percent) students agreed that they had TV set at home and watch television at the sitting room. About 186 (77.5 percent) students did not agree that they watch TV in their bedrooms.

Quantitative results were confirmed by findings from the one-to-one interview and FGDs also known as group interviews. During interviews, most of the teachers explained that majority of the students had access to television because most of the residents were business people, employed, and entrepreneurs who were able to buy TV sets. There were some farmers who could manage to possess a TV set. During FGDs` with parents, it was revealed that most of the households possessed TV sets. Parents and teachers explained that they watch TV in the sitting room with their children. Few parents possessed more than one TV set and allow their children to watch TV in their bedrooms but were not aware of what children watch when alone. Parents and the teachers' opinions on students' accessibility to the television were quoted. A parent in FGD said: "We, parents watch TV with our children at the sitting room. Neither of us have TV in bedrooms because our economic status does not allow to have more than one TV sets. Children also watch TV at neighbours' house, TV public halls and showrooms."[1]

Another parent in FGD added: "At home, we have two TV sets. One is placed at the sitting room and another in our bedroom. We have a Form One secondary school child and two primary school children who watch TV with us at sitting room. Before, boys had one in their room but we removed it because we found that they prefer watching TV to studying."[2]

One head of school through interview said:

> Nowadays, television is not a luxury asset. It is a family's need for getting information about the world. But our adolescents I think, they are not using it properly. Some parents do come to us complaining that their children are not doing any school work at home. What they can do is watching television. You see! A day before yesterday a parent of a Form Three girl came to me complaining that her daughter watches television all night long. Her parent has talked to her several times but she never stopped. Her mother decided to take the cables away. Surprisingly, after two days the girl had her own cables. Now, what is she watching at night alone?[3]

These findings are in line with other studies done in America and elsewhere. For example, a study by Groebel revealed that about 91 percent of the children in America had access to a TV set primarily at home, and about 83 percent of the school going

---

1. Female Parent associated with School B, interviewed on 14/7/2014.
2. Male Parent associated with School D, interviewed on 16/7/2014.
3. Headmistress of School E, interviewed on 10/7/2014.

children in Africa had access to TV set at home.[4] The accessibility of students to TV in Africa is not static and it has increased a lot.

The findings also concur with that of Nielsen who found 54 percent of respondents had access to more than three or more TV sets, 28 percent had two TV sets, whereas 18 percent had only one TV set at home.[5] Myer points out that about 99.2 percent of the children in industrialized countries have access to TV set and most of homes have more than one TV sets.[6] Hence, the disparity in students' accessibilities to TV in the world regions is a result of different economic levels of the households and the region's developments.

In this study the researcher discovered that many middle income households had TV sets in their sitting rooms. Parents with high income provided TV sets to their children in their bedrooms. This indicates high probability of accessing television. In Africa and Tanzania in particular, TV sets are more or less placed and watched at the sitting rooms. Roberts, Foehr, and Rideout confirm that in America majority of the adolescents have TV sets in their own bedrooms.[7] This concur with what has been explained in chapter two that in the developed world regions there is a high accessibility of children to television as households possess more than one TV set. Therefore, based on this findings it is quite right to say that the more the increase of higher income earning class the more the increase of Children's accessibility to TV and other media at large. Obviously, the higher accessibility to television leads to the higher accessibility to violent TV programs.

4. Groebel, "The UNESCO Global Study on Media Violence" (1998).
5. Nielsen, "Home Accessibility to TV" (2009).
6. Myers, *Social Psychology* (2010).
7. Roberts, Foehr, & Rideout, *Generation M* (2005).

Violent TV Programs and the Amount of Time Secondary School Children Spend on Them

Under this objective the researcher aimed at ascertaining violent TV programs and the amount of time spent by the children watching such violent programs. In order to obtain data, a questionnaire was administered to students. Data were also obtained through qualitative measure that involved one-to-one interview with teachers and FDGs with parents. Qualitative data were used as confirmatory measure on the information gathered from the field questionnaires.

Violent television programs

This subsection was important because the researcher wanted to identify the TV programs with violent acts that were watched by secondary school children. The children were provided with questionnaires which asked them to identify types of TV programs and the violent acts they watched. The results obtained from children are summarized in Table 4.2.

Table 4.2: Children's Responses on Identifying Violent TV Programs with Acts (N=240)

		Agree		Uncertain		Disagree	
S/N	Items	f	%	f	%	f	%
1	Television drama programs: sexual acts, theft, killings, slaps, shootings, drug and substance use, terrorist acts, brutality, interpersonal violence.	219	91.3	02	0.8	19	7.1
2	Television movies programs: half naked attire style, humiliation, killings, fighting, robbery, and sexual acts	231	96.2	00	00	09	3.8

Hearing Research Data

S/N	Items	Agree f	%	Uncertain f	%	Disagree f	%
3	Television Music programs: males put on earrings, women in half naked style, sexual harassment, violent songs	224	93.4	04	1.7	12	05
4	Television sports and games programs: heavy weight boxing matches, wrestling, hitting, shoving, punching, fighting, and verbal abuse	209	87.1	01	0.4	30	12.5
5	Television informational programs: murders, suicides, wars, fighting, religious and political violence	219	91.3	01	0.4	20	08

Source: Field Data

Table 4.2 shows that 231 (96.2 percent) secondary school children agreed that television movies programs had violent acts such as humiliation, killings, fighting, robbery, and sexual acts. About 224 (93.4 percent) children agreed that television music programs are violent, and acts being watched in it include sexual harassments, verbal abuse, and violent songs.

These quantitative results were confirmed by qualitative findings. During FGD sessions, most of the parents articulated that in television movies and in the music programs there are many violent acts which most of them are observed and imitated by their secondary school children. A parent in FGD said:

> I think secondary school children like most to watch television movie programs. In TV movies, I find my children watch violent acts such as mass killing, love affairs, fighting, slaps, interpersonal conflict, suicides, robbery, prostitution, and humiliation. When I am at home I usually watch with them and tell them to change the channel when the TV scene displays love affairs because children observe and like to practice immediately or later.[8]

8. Male Parent associated with School A, interviewed on 28/7/ 2014.

A guardian in FGD added saying: "My children spend more time in watching TV movie and music programs than watching educational programs. Most of the time, children like most to watch TV programs with fighting, mass killing, boxing, violent lyrics, interpersonal conflicts and language abuse. As a parent, I discourage my children to watch such TV programs because they have great influence to our children."[9]

During interview with teachers, it was also reported that television movies and music programs had plenty of violent acts. A teacher through interview had this to say before the researcher:

> There are many television programs with violent acts which have great influence on our secondary school children. These include television movies, drama, comedy, music, sports and games, and informational programs. The most violent television programs I know are music, movies, and drama. The violent acts from three programs are watched much, imitated and practiced by children may be because their media role models are either rewarded or not punished for the violent behaviors exhibited by them.[10]

From these findings it can be deduced that, TV programs with violent acts are watched by children. Parents do not want their children to watch violent TV programs. Parents believe that these programs can negatively affect their children's behaviors. Teachers also reported that violent acts performed by attractive models in TV programs have great influence on children who identify with them.

These findings concur with Bandura's Social Learning Perspective of modeling and reinforcement who found that children imitate the role model who is a powerful character, rewarded rather than punished for the behavior, and share characteristic with children.[11] This is also similar to Pretorius who conducted a study on

9. Female Guardian associated with School C, interviewed, 8/7/2014).
10. Second master of School F, interviewed on 5/7/2014).
11. Bandura, *Self-efficacy* (1977).

violence in South African children's TV programs and found that TV movies or film programs had characters that kill, injure, and fight each other.[12] These characters exhibited aggressive behaviors which were being observed and imitated by school going students. On the other hand, some children become more fearful and full of anxiety as they perceived that violent TV world was similar to the real world violence.[13] Similarly, other studies indicate that television movies, music and drama programs were the most violent and hurt school going children to a great extent.[14] The findings of this study indicate that students are extremely aware of the effect of TV violence watching despite the fact that there is no formal class on such knowledge. For this reason, parents and teachers have to guide these children on selecting non-violent TV programs.

Amount of time children spent on watching violent TV programs

The sub-objective sought to ascertain the amount of time students spend on watching violent TV per day and per week. The summary of the findings are presented in Table 4.3.

---

12. Pretorius, "Violence in South African" (2006).
13. Gerbner, G. "Reclaim our Cultural Mythology" (1994).
14. Anderson, et al. "The Influence of Media Violence" (2003); Rawlings, "Reaching an Agreement" (2011); Nevins, "The Effect of Media" (2004).

The Impact of Watching Violent Television Programs

Table 4.3: Amount of Time Students Spent on
Watching Violent TV Programs (N=240)

	Hours									
	1-3		4-6		7-9		10+		Total	
Days	f	%	f	%	f	%	f	%	f	%
Monday to Friday	170	71	68	28	2	1	-	-	240	100
Saturday	40	17	97	41	82	34	21	8	240	100
Sunday	45	19	50	21	96	40	49	20	240	100

Source: Field Data

Table 4.3 indicates that the amount of time spent by students during the week days differs from the weekend days. As Table 4.3 shows, from Monday to Friday 170 (71 percent) students watch TV violence for a maximum of three hours, which is equivalent to 15 hours for five days. On Saturday, about 97 (41 percent) students used six hours, whereas on Sunday, about 96 (40 percent) students used nine hours watching violence on television programs. This is to say, students spent an average of seven-and-half hours on weekend days watching violent TV programs per day. Thus students who spend three hours in week days and seven-and-half hours on weekends watching violent TV programs are noted to spend an average of five-and-quarter hours watching TV violence per day, that is, more than 35 hours per week.

The findings in this study are similar to previous studies which show that, students spend between three to five hours watching violent TV programs per day or 21 to 35 hours per week.[15] Such hours for a school going children to spend on watching violent programs might not only have significant effect to their school performance and discipline but also home chores. In the similar vein, Thompson and Austin argue that students who watch violent TV programs such as movies, drama, and music more than

15. Groebel, "The UNESCO Global Study Media Violence" (1999); Graham, *How Television Viewing Affect* (2006); Gentile, Saleem, & Anderson, "Public Policy" (2007); Daniyal, & Hassan, "The Impact of Television" (2013).

10 hours or so in a week their class works become affected and thus achieved worse grade.[16] Having manifested to what extent violent TV programs affect school going children's performance, American Academy of Pediatrics recommends that adolescent secondary school children should not watch violent TV programs even for one or two hours.[17] Therefore, this suggests that students are not recommended to watch violent television programs extensively. The reason behind is that the more children spend on watching violent TV programs the more they are likely to score worse grades.

Ways through which Watching Violent TV Programs Affects Secondary School Children's Academic Performance

The ways through which watching violent TV programs affect the academic performance of the secondary school children was determined quantitatively and qualitatively. Children filled in the questionnaire by responding at either Yes or No. Findings obtained through interview and FGDs with teachers and parents respectively served to further explain the findings obtained through questionnaire. This objective was subdivided into two research questions.

Ways through which watching violent TV programs affects secondary school children's academic performance

This section presents and discusses ways through which watching violent TV programs affects children's school academic performance. These ways are essential as the researcher wanted to determine how watching violent TV programs affect students' academic performance. The summary of the quantitative results are presented in Table 4.4.

16. Thompson, & Austin, "Television Viewing" (2003).
17. American Academy Pediatrics, "AAP Policy Statement" (2001).

The Impact of Watching Violent Television Programs

Table 4.4: Children's Responses on Ways through which Watching Violent TV Programs affect their Academic Performance (N=240)

S/N	Items	Yes f	%	No f	%	Total f	%
1	Truancy	211	88	29	12	240	100
2	School dropout	184	76.5	56	23.5	240	100
3	Displacement of time	237	99	3	1	240	100
4	Decrease in intellectual thinking capacity	108	45	132	55	240	100
5	Increase in suspensions or expulsion from school	198	82.6	42	17.4	240	100
6	Practicing anti-social behavior at home and school premises	232	96.7	8	3.3	240	100

Source: Field Data

Table 4.4 shows that 237 (99 percent) secondary school children agreed that watching violent TV programs affects their academic performance by displacement of time, which means that every hour spent by children watching violent TV programs is an hour not spent for studying. About 232 (96.7 percent) secondary school children agreed that watching violent TV programs affects their academic performance by practicing anti-social behavior at home and/or at school premises. However, about 132 (55 percent) students did not agree that the decrease in intellectual thinking capacity is caused by watching violent TV programs and that it affects the academic performance of the secondary school children.

During the FGD sessions with parents and one-to-one interview with teachers, it was revealed that displacement of time was the foremost way that affects secondary school children's academic performance. One of the teachers during the interview said:

> Displacement of time or shift is the greatest enemy of the students' academic progress. A student who misuses time through watching violent TV programs is likely to kill himself/herself academically. For a student to spend more than three hours per day in a week he/she

is misusing parents' fund; and to intervene the situation parents and teachers have to play their role by guiding their children properly.[18]

One of the parents during FGD sessions added by saying:

> I have two secondary school children; a girl in Form Four and a boy in Form Three. The boy stays watching violent TV programs most of his time while the girl spends less time watching TV violence. If my son is not monitored properly, neither does the school assignments nor household chores. Academically, nowadays my son performs below average while his sister does well. It is obvious that television violence watching consumes a lot of time of the viewers.[19]

The findings suggest that watching violent TV programs for three hours or so per day leads students to perform poorly in academics. For this reason, teachers and parents need to have good strategies to let students utilize their time for studies so as to do well in academics.

During one-to-one interview with teachers and the FGDs with parents, it was revealed that practicing anti-social behaviors at home and at school premises is a way through which watching violent TV programs affects academic performance of the students. One of the parents in FGD said:

> I have a Form Two son who likes most to watch television violence and is fond of watching boxing, karate, and Kung fu. The boy fights a lot at school and at home. Two times I was called by teachers to discuss about his fights and stealing other's properties. At home he sells family properties to outsiders, fights against elder sisters and brothers, and even argues with us without any fear.[20]

In an interview with one teacher, he said that:

---

18. Second Master from School F Interviewed on 7/7/2014.
19. Male Parent Associated with School B Interviewed on 25/7/2014.
20. Female Parent Associated with School C, interviewed on 14/7/2014.

Students who misbehave at school are also misbehaving at home. In case of watching violent TV programs, students watch and learn what attracts them from the television role models. If students identify themselves with role models who behave violently and are not punished are likely to imitate the behavior. These students are the ones who do not practice prosocial behavior at school and at home premises and mostly they perform poorly in academics.[21]

The findings of this study are similar with findings in other studies conducted in Sub-Saharan Africa and elsewhere. For example, a study conducted by Barlett, Anderson, and Swing on video game effects revealed that playing too much video games hurts students' school performance by displacement of time.[22] Basing on this argument then beyond doubt also watching too much non-violent and violent TV programs hurt school performance by displacement of time since the issues here is the amount of time spent on media and nothing else. This means that the time for doing class work assignments, private study, and group discussions is spent on watching violent TV programs. So, watching TV violence steals time for studying and thus lowers the students' academic performance.

Apart from students spending much time on watching TV violence instead of studying, they also engage in practicing antisocial behavior at school and at home premises. The findings are in line with those of Nevins who explored on the effect of media violence adolescent on youth and found that secondary school youth disobey parents' advice on performing home chores and engage in antisocial acts such as robbery, fighting, and causing a lot of violence at home and school premises.[23] It is argued that any person who spoils the peace of the society by engaging on violent acts is likely to be jailed.[24] Consequently, students who practice

---

21. Academic Mistress from School D, interviewed on 31/7/2014.
22. Barlett, Anderson, & Swing, "Video Game Effects" (2009).
23. Nevins, "The Effect of Media" (2004).
24. Baron, Branscombe, & Byrne, *Social Psychology* (2009).

antisocial behavior are also likely to face imprisonment, and by that time they will not be studying anymore.

Impact of watching violent TV programs to the children's Academic Performance

The study also determined the impact of watching violent TV programs on academic performance of students. The summary of the findings are presented in Table 4.5

Table 4.5: Impact of Watching Violent TV Programs to the Children's Academic Performance (N=240)

S/N	Items	Yes f	Yes %	No f	No %	Total f	Total %
1	Decreases children's GPA	231	96	09	4	240	100
2	Children depend much on teachers in academic affairs	184	76.5	56	23.5	240	100
3	Lowers children's efficient and effectiveness in doing class assignments	228	95	12	05	240	100
4	Poor achievement of children' educational goals	198	82.5	42	17.5	240	100
5	Increases children's grade point average	11	4.6	229	95.4	240	100

Source: Field Data

Note: GPA=Grade Point Average, f=frequency

As indicated in Table 4.5, watching violent TV programs decreases secondary school children's grade point average, and lowers students' efficient and effectiveness of doing class assignments. Table 4.5 shows that about 231 (96 percent) of students agreed that watching violent TV programs decreases the grade point average of the school children. About 228 (95 percent) of students agreed that low students' efficient and effectiveness of doing class assignments is an effect of watching violent TV programs. Generally, all items except one were agreed by most of the students that TV violence watching has effect on the academic performance of the students. Yet, when school children spent the same amount of time watching non-violent TV programs their performance suffered as well. On the other hand, 229 (95.4 percent) of students did not agree that watching TV violence increased the grade point average of the students. Hence, the two agreed items and the disagreed are discussed in detail underneath.

Findings from FGDs with parents and one-to-one interview with teachers revealed that watching violent TV programs affected children's academics negatively. Children who watch violent TV programs several times extensively, their academic progress in school decreased. One of the second mistresses through interview had this to say: "TV violence watching has a great effect to the grade point average of the students. Students who spend a lot of time watching TV violence have less time for doing homework and group discussions, and this lead them to score low grades in internal and external examinations."[25]

A parent in a FGD had this to say:

> It is really painful to have a son who doesn't pay attention to the parents' advice. My son is a Form Two and is addicted to watching TV violence. In our absence, he watches TV all the daylong and never performs home responsibilities and school homework. The subject mean average of the first term dropped down and shocked both of us, me and my husband. We don't know which will be the right way of rescuing him.[26]

Low students' efficient and effectiveness was also reported during FGDs and one-to-one interviews as the impact of watching violent TV programs on academic performance of the children. Parents and teachers' opinions were quoted. One of the academic masters through interview had this to say: "Violent TV programs teaches bad behavior to our students. Once students develop the behavior of watching violent TV programs extensively, they become

---

25. Second Mistress from School C, interviewed on 14/7/2014.
26. Female Parent Associated with School E, interviewed on 12/6/2014.

very stubborn. Many are disruptive in class, fail to do their class assignments, collect the exercise book with incomplete assignments and several times they are forced to do the corrections."[27]

Again a parent in a FGD confirmed:"My Form One son spends much of his time watching TV programs. Teachers reported that your son neither does well in individual class assignments nor participates in group assignments. All his class works are both incomplete and poorly done or not corrected. Worse enough your son leaves lessons to watching violence on TV in a school nearby public hall and showroom. We were truly shocked."[28]

These findings also revealed that the more time spent on watching violent TV programs the more the decrease of students' grade point average and the lower the students' efficient and effectiveness of doing class assignments. However, grade point average would also decrease when students spent the same amount of hours watching non-violent TV programs per day in a week.

Students' information on academic performance in relation to the amount of time spent on watching violent TV programs was obtained through documentary review. Students' academic performance was determined according to the secondary school grading system, which then, was cross tabulated against hours students spent on watching violent TV programs. The summary of the findings are presented in Table 4.6.

Table 4.6: The Relationship between Children's Grade Scores and the Time Spent on Watching Violent TV Programs (N=240)

Hours / Day	Grades							
	A		B+		B		C	
	f	%	f	%	f	%	f	%
1-3	-	-	1	0.4	1	0.4	2	0.8
4-6	-	-	-	-	-	-	-	-
Total	-	-	1	0.4	1	0.4	2	0.8

27. Academic Master from School D, interviewed on 18/7/2014.
28. Male Parent Associated with School E, interviewed on 12/6/2014.

The Impact of Watching Violent Television Programs

Hours / Day	Grades							
	A		B+		B		C	
	f	%	f	%	f	%	f	%
7-9	-	-	-	-	-	-	-	-
10+	-	-	-	-	-	-	-	-
Total	-	-	1	0.4	1	0.4	2	0.8

Hours / Day	Grades							
	D		E		F		Total	
	f	%	f	%	f	%	f	%
1-3	11	4.6	22	9.2	48	20	85	35.4
4-6	1	0.4	3	1.4	68	28.2	72	30
7-9	-	-	2	0.8	58	24.2	60	25
10+	-	-	1	0.4	22	9.2	23	9.6
Total	12	5	28	11.8	196	81.6	240	100

Source: Field Data

Note: A (75-100), B+ (60-74), B (50-59), C (40-49), D (30-39), E (21-29), F (0-20); f=frequency

Table 4.6 indicates that 68 (28.2 percent) secondary school children who spent four to six hours per day watching violent TV programs scored F grade; and only 4 (1.8 percent) students scored grade D and E. About 58 (24.2 percent) students who spent seven to nine hours per day watching violent TV programs also scored F grade. About 48 (20 percent) secondary school children who spent one to three hours per day watching violent TV programs scored grade F, while 37 (15.4 percent) students passed the exam and scored from B+ to E grade. Therefore, this table indicates that secondary school children who watch violent TV programs for more than three hours a day perform poorly in their academic arena.

The findings through documentary review revealed that watching violent TV programs affect secondary school children's performance in a negative way. Table 4.6 discloses that the number of secondary school children's score grades decreases in relative to the increase amount of time children spent on watching violent TV programs. This agrees with media displacement hypothesis which states that "playing and/or watching media displace time on other activities."[29] Therefore, this study document that the more the increase in the amount of time that a secondary school child spends on watching violent TV programs per day the more the decrease in his/her academic performance.

The findings of this study are in line with other several studies. For example, Slotsve, Carmen, Sarver, and Villareal-Watkins found that watching violent TV programs steals time related to success in school and causing the students to score low grade point average.[30] Barr-Anderson, Van den Berg, Neumark-Sztainer, and Story also found that students who watch TV violence more than three hours per day did worse at school and were twice likely not to continue their education past high school since they had low grade point average.[31] Moreover, the findings concur with that of Cummings and Vandewater who studied on the relationship of adolescent video game play to time spent in other activities comprising a sample size of 1491 youth between the ages of 10 and 19. They found that "gamers spent 30 percent less time reading and 34 percent less time doing homework"[32] The same applies to secondary school children who watch violent TV programs more than three hour per day spent less time reading and less time doing homework. This means that spending high amount of time playing video game and watching violent TV programs hurts school performance to a great extent, and consequently decreases the grade point average. However, spending the same amount of time watching non-violence TV would also have similar effect on students' academic performance. Kirkorian, Wartella, and Anderson had the view that since violent TV content is linked with a poorer quality of cognitive development and worse academic achievement, producers

29. Cummings, & Vandewater, "Relation of Adolescent," 684.

30. Slotsve, Carmen, Sarver, & Villareal, "Television Violence," 26.

31. Barr-Anderson, et al., "Characteristics Associated with Older Adolescent," 718.

32. Cummings, & Vandewater, "Relation of Adolescent," 685.

and parents can take steps to make use of positive effects of media and lessen the negative effects.[33] Therefore, spending much time on both violent and non-violent TV programs has negative effect not only to the secondary school children but also to all school going children, and the college and university students.

The findings in the current study also revealed that a substantial number of students 229 (95.4 percent) did not agree that watching violent TV programs increases the grade point average of the students who watch such programs. This means that spending a lot of time watching TV violence does not contribute to better academic performance of the students. The more time students spent watching violent TV programs the less time spent on class works, private studies, and group work participation. Similarly, other social scientists argue that students who spent more time watching television or violent television programs than concentrating with studies hardly complete the class assignments and score good grades.[34] Thus, this study documents that there is a negative relationship between the time spent on TV violence watching and academic performance of the students.

The findings also concur with those of Thompson and Austin who found that watching either violent or non-violent television programs more than 10 hours in a week can lead students to perform their class works below the standard.[35] The same observation was made by Borzekowski and Robinson who noted that students who spend more time watching TV or violent television spend less time on homework, and participate less in group assignments, which lead them to score poorer on standardized tests and finally end with a very low grade point average. In addition, late-night television violence watching tires school going children out so that they can't pay attention in schools and this paves a way to

---

33. Kirkorian, Wartella, & Anderson, "Children and Electronic Media," 39.

34. Anderson, et al., "The Influence of Media" (2003); Borzekowski, & Robinson, "The Household Media Environment" (2005); Barr-Anderson, et al., "Characteristic Associated with Older" (2008).

35. Thompson, & Austin, "Television Viewing" (2003).

score low-grade point average.[36] Therefore, the much time spent by secondary school children on watching violent TV programs the worst grade they score.

Impact of Watching Violent TV Programs to the Secondary School Children's Discipline

Under this objective the researcher was interested in finding out the disciplinary problems of the students imitated from TV violence role models, which they reproduce in the real world. This was measured both quantitatively and qualitatively. Quantitative measure involved a questionnaire which assessed the effect of TV violence watching on the discipline of the students on a five point likert scale. The responses ranged from strongly agree to strongly disagree. The findings are summarized in Table 4.7.

Table 4.7: Children's Responses on Identifying the Impact of Watching Violent TV Programs on Discipline (N=240)

S/N	Items	Agree f	Agree %	Uncertain f	Uncertain %	Disagree f	Disagree %
1	Fight at school and home	166	69	4	2	70	29
2	Use abusive language	221	92	2	1	17	7
3	Often argue and try to fight with teachers	89	37	-	-	151	63
4	Initiate school violence	173	72	3	1.3	64	26.7
5	Steal other's properties	184	76.6	-	-	56	23.4
6	Engage in love affairs	214	89.2	1	0.4	25	10.4
7	Truancy	132	55	-	-	108	45
8	Often disobey elders and parents	146	61	1	0.4	93	38.6
9	Engage in drug abuse	209	87.1	1	0.4	30	12.5

Source: Field Data

36. Borzekowski, & Robinson, "The Household Media" (2005).

The Impact of Watching Violent Television Programs

Table 4.7 indicates that 221 (92 percent) of secondary school children agreed that the use of abusive language by them is the impact of watching violent TV programs. About 214 (89.2 percent) students also agreed that engagement of students in love affairs was also an impact of watching violent TV programs. Other impact of watching violent TV programs agreed by secondary school children include stealing other's properties, initiating of school violence, and fighting at school and home. On the other hand about 151 (63 percent) students did not agree that students who watch TV violence often argue and try to fight with teachers.

Qualitative findings showed that watching violent TV programs had impact on the discipline of the students. For instance, students who watch violent TV programs were noted to use abusive language and engage in love affairs. They also indicated that there were very few students who dare to argue and fight with their teachers. A discipline master through interview had this to say:

> Abusive words directed to their fellow students are not imaginable. Abusive language experienced among secondary school children includes insults like stupid, garbage, son of a bitch and fool; and some are related to male and female reproductive organs. Such students think that abusive language is normal while it is not. On the other hand, abusive language is harshly used against each other when they are nearly to fight or soon after their fight.[37]

Not only that, but also a parent in FGD confirmed:

> The abusive language uttered by students is terribly astonishing. I think as they observe and imitate TV role models and people around them they learn how to abuse peers, opposite sex, and the younger ones. Nowadays abusive language among youngsters is normalized and has become part of their culture. These include foolish, fuck you, stupid, idiot, loser, and other related to parents' bodily functions.[38]

---

37. Discipline Master from School A, interviewed on 25/7/2014.
38. Male Parent associated with School D, interviewed on 18/7/2014.

Hearing Research Data

In addition to that, a guardian in a FGD complained:

> My Form Three son had a TV set in his bedroom. One midnight the TV was on with a low voice then I told him to switch off the TV and concentrate on studying. When I asked him in the morning he said that he was watching the movies. After a month, one day in the late midnight he also turned on the TV at a low voice and watching the movies with love affair contents. The boy started scoring low grades, and at the end of the year he impregnated a classmate and both were expelled from school....[39]

Similarly, a head of school through interview had this say:

> It is indeed unfortunate that some students do not pay attention to our advice on how to succeed in academics. They have their own teachers in TV violence who teach sexual violence that they pay attention to and understand them well and put into use. They engage in love affairs without afraid of early pregnancies, contacting sexual transmitted diseases such as HIV/AIDS, gonorrhea, syphilis, and Chlamydia. It is really painful when girls become pregnant, hence, terminated from their studies.[40]

Findings obtained through documentary review showed that, school authorities were using educational law of Tanzania number 25 of 1978 from circular number 5 of 2011 which articulates disciplinary problems with measures to be taken.[41] Therefore, secondary school children who were found with disciplinary problems were either suspended or terminated from school. The findings of documentary review are presented in Table 4.8.

---

39. Female Guardian associated with School A, interviewed on 14/7/2014.
40. Headmaster from School E, interviewed on 4/8/2014.
41. MoEVT, "Educational Law of Tanzania" (2011).

Table 4.8: Children's Frequency of Disciplinary Problems reported with Actions taken by School Authorities

S/N	Disciplinary Problems	Schools						Actions Taken		Total
		A	B	C	D	E	F	Sn	Tn	
1	Pregnancy	1	3	1	1	2	2	-	10	10
2	Engaging in love affairs	6	11	4	8	10	3	42	-	42
3	Truancy (90 days) consecutively	2	6	2	1	1	2	-	14	14
4	Truancy (30 days) consecutively	9	13	1	5	11	9	48	-	48
5	Drug abuse and substance use	5	8	-	-	1	1	-	15	15
6	Theft	13	9	7	6	9	5	49	-	49
7	Fighting at school	3	8	1	1	1	5	12	7	19
8	Initiating school boycott	1	2	-	-	1	-	-	4	4
9	Leaving school premises without permission	10	21	8	12	6	1	58	-	58
Total		50	81	24	34	42	28	209	50	259

Source: Field Data

Note: Sn= Suspension, TN=Termination.

As indicated in Table 4.8, it was found that 209 secondary school children were suspended while 50 students were terminated from school due to their disciplinary problems. School B had 81 children who had disciplinary problems whereas school A had 50 students. Thus, the two schools are assumed to have children who watch violent TV programs at length and what they have observed and imitated they reproduce them at school premise and possibly at home to.

The findings revealed that secondary school children who watch violent TV programs with abusive language accept and regularize the use of such language against their fellow children and peers. The same applies to the students who were fond of watching TV programs with sexual violence. They had high possibilities of engaging in love affairs with opposite sex peers, classmates and their home friends. This falls under Bandura's Social Learning Theory, as students watch violent TV programs with abusive language and sexual violence, they observe and imitate violent acts performed by the attractive model and the motivation along with them and then reproduce them later.[42]

Findings of this study are similar to the findings of the study conducted in United States by Hargrave who found that school going children exposed to abusive language in such media accept it as part of their youth culture, which reduces their inhibition about using it themselves.[43] Abuse language includes: toilet humour-body parts; profane language such as ass, hell, damn; bad language like suck and butt; abusive yelling; motherfucker, and girlfucker; and bastard. Hargrave also found that such bad language influenced verbal and physical aggression to the victims. [44]

With regard to love affairs, findings of this study are also similar to Myer's who found that youth who watch high amount of sexual violence on television may acquire sexual scripts which lead them to perform in their real life relationships. Myer also points out that school youth perceive their peers as sexually active to develop sexual active attitudes; to experience early intercourse as a result they come into contact with sexual transmitted diseases, and early and unplanned pregnancies.[45] Hence, secondary school children who consistently watch violent TV programs observe and imitate aggressive and other anti-social behaviors exhibited by TV role models and reproduce them in the similar situation.

---

42. Bandura, *Social Foundations of Thought* (1986).
43. Hargrave, "Bad Language in Television" (2008).
44. Ibid.
45. Myer, *Social Psychology* (2010).

Parents/ Guardians' Role in Addressing the Impact of Watching Violent TV Programs to Secondary School Children

This objective was intended to examine the day to day roles of the parents in addressing the impact of watching violent TV programs on their secondary school children. This objective was measured both quantitatively and qualitatively. Quantitative measure involved a questionnaire which was administered to the secondary school children who responded to express parents and/or guardians' roles to address the impact of watching violent TV programs to them. The questionnaire examined the frequency on the role of parents in addressing the impact of watching violent TV programs on the five point likert scale measure, which ranged from strongly agree to strongly disagree. Qualitative part involved FGDs with parents. The findings are summarized in Table 4.9.

Table 4.9: Children's Responses on Parents' Role in Addressing the Impact of Watching Violent TV Programs (N=240)

S/N	Items	Agree f	%	Uncertain f	%	Disagree f	%	Total f	%
1	Limit me from watching TV violence	214	89.3	1	0.4	25	10.4	240	100
2	Discourage me to watch TV violence	231	96.2	-	-	9	3.8	240	100
3	Keep TV out of my bedroom	212	88.3	2	0.8	26	10.9	240	100
4	Ban outright violent TV programs	184	77	8	3	48	20	240	100
5	Choose appropriate TV programs for me	228	95.1	-	-	12	4.9	240	100
6	Join me to watch TV violence and discuss its effects	66	27.5	1	0.4	173	72.1	240	100

Source: Field Data

Table 4.9 indicates that 231 (96.2 percent) secondary school children agreed that parents discouraged them to watch violent TV programs. Two hundred and twenty eight (95.1 percent) secondary school children agreed that when parents found them watching violent TV programs decided to choose appropriate TV programs for them. Moreover, 214 (89.2 percent) secondary school children agreed that when parents found them watching violent TV programs limit them from watching TV violence. On the other hand, 173 (72.1 percent) secondary school children did not agree that parents joined them to watch TV violence and discuss its effects. These four items are discussed extensively below.

It was revealed that most parents discourage their secondary school children to watch violent TV programs for the fear that their behavior will be diverted. However, parents expressed that secondary school students have many opportunities of watching violent TV programs if they are discouraged at home. They would go to neighbours' house where parents do not discourage them to watch TV violence. Some decided to go to TV show rooms, and public halls to watch with peers, friends and school mates. Secondary school students were tricky and aware of the hours at which violent TV programs are in air. A guardian in a FGD had this to say:

> I have two boys, a Form One and a Form Three student. One day, at 22 hours when everyone was supposed to go for sleep, these boys requested to have two hours more for studying at our sitting room. At 23 hours I got up and opened my door very gently and I found them watching movies with love affairs content and I commanded them switch off the TV and go to sleep. And the next term I decided to send them to a boarding secondary school.[46]

Another parent in a FGD added saying: "One day evening I found my Form Four son with his friends watching TV drama programs with sexual violence, slaps, interpersonal violence, and killings, imperatively I told him turn off the TV and no more watching TV in our absent."[47] Furthermore, parents' role of choos-

46. Female Guardian associated with School F, interviewed on 24/7/2014.
47. Male Parent associated with School C, interviewed on 14/7/2014.

ing appropriate TV programs for their secondary school children who were found watching violence on television was agreed by most of the students. The findings revealed that parents decided to choose appropriate programs for their students. Most of the parents argued that instead of watching violent TV programs students should be watching other things that might have more educational and disciplinary benefits. A parent recommended appropriate programs along with channels for school going children. The summary of the findings are presented in Table 4.10.

Table 4.10: Parents' Appropriate Programs Chosen for their Secondary School Children

S/N	TV Programs	Channel
1	Educational programs	
	Skonga	EATV
	Jifunze lugha Yetu (Learn our Language)	TBC
	Malumbano ya Hoja (Dialogue/debate on Certain educational topic)	ITV
	Students subject periods (Math, History, Biology . . .)	TBC2
2	This week in perspective program	TBC
3	Maisha Plus	ITV
4	Informational programs	All
5	Religious programs	Immanuel & Agape TV
		Azam TV
6	Health programs	ATV, DTV, TBC

Source: Field Data

Table 4.10 indicates that parents allow their children to watch appropriate TV programs which include educational, informational, religious, and health programs. This means that the programs are beneficial to children's school performance, moral conduct, and health. The findings of this study also confirm that secondary school children should not be allowed to watch violent TV programs except informational, sports and games. The rationale for allowing students to watch TV informational programs was to let them become familiar with current issues about the world; whereas TV sports and games programs were found beneficial for children to learn skills, for physical protection and that they provide employment in future. The parents' day to day role when they find student children watching violent TV programs were quoted. A parent said:

> Two times I found my Form Two girl watching, and playing rock music and 'bongo fleva.' Two times I commanded to switch off the TV. After a week I requested her teachers to send me her academic progress report. The report sent described her bad behavior and poor grades she scored. I talked to her about the report content and told her no more playing your favourite music, and other violent TV programs.[48]

Another parent in a FGD added saying: "The first time I found my Form One son with his classmates watching movies with sexual violence I warned them not to repeat again elsewhere. Later, I talked to my children that TV will be switched on in our presence and only an hour is enough for you all per day."[49] The findings show that parents are in the same line with teachers who recommended that parents should put a TV set out of reach in their absence at home; convening public advocacy for educating neighbours and others on the impact of watching violent TV programs on the academic performance and discipline of the secondary school children; and providing education to students of all ages and the means to overcome the problem. Teachers' suggestion calls for addressing the problem to all people including children themselves, parents, teachers, neighbours, TV public halls and TV show rooms owners and TV industry people in order to save our school going children. Parents alone cannot overcome this problem.

Findings on the parents' role of addressing the impact of watching violent TV programs are similar to the findings of other studies conducted outside Africa. For instance, research studies

---

48. Female Guardian associated with School E, interviewed on 12/06/2014.
49. Male Parent associated with School A, interviewed on 14/07/2014.

found that parents discourage their children to watch TV violence and encouraged children to be critical of the message they encounter when watching non-violent TV and violent TV programs in their presence.[50] So, discouragement to watch violent TV programs and encouraging children to act as filters of the messages represented on them aim at rescuing them from significant risks patterning to watching the programs.

Centerwall argues that parents should not only be choosing appropriate TV programs for their secondary school children but also guiding what their children should watch on TV and how much.[51] This means that the content of TV should be known by parents who have to decide which content is good for their children. American Academy Pediatrics reminds that there should be a standard package which states that 'less TV is better, and violent TV is the worst and should not be watched' by school going children.[52] Moreover, American Academy Pediatrics is very much concerned for rescuing children from deleterious impacts caused by watching violent TV programs and suggests that "office counseling has been shown to be effective."[53] Hence, the suggestion will be productive only when parents are responsible for their children and whenever possible send them to the counselors and at the same time guiding school going children to spend less time on non-violent TV programs and no time on watching television violence.

Another standard package is that 'this is TV-Free Area' meaning that at home children's bedrooms should be free from TV and/or violent television.[54] In addition, Centerwall suggests that the appropriate way of discouraging children's exposure to TV violent programs is to emphasize time channel locks, program rating system, and education of the public regarding good viewing

---

50. Huesmann, & Taylor, "The Role of Media" (2006); Gentile, Saleem, & Anderson, "Public Policy" 2007.
51. Centerwall, "Exposure to Television" (1992).
52. American Academy Pediatrics. "Media Violence" (2009).
53. Ibid.
54. Ibid.

habits.[55] Hence, this awakens parents to have a specific area fit for all to watch TV programs and when and how much to watch and watching suitable TV programs only.

Adversely, majority of students did not agree that their parents will join them to watch violent TV programs and discuss its effect. Parents confirm that they do not watch TV violence with their children except informational, sports and games. The findings of this study also concur with that of Huesmann, Moise-Titus, Podolski, and Eron who found that parents faced difficulties to control completely what children watch in televisions especially when children access violent TV programs in bedrooms. Moreover, they suggested that more informed legal debate is needed on this subject because broadcasters and program markers cannot avoid all responsibility for what children are exposed to.[56] Huesmann and Taylor assert that children whose parents discuss with them the impact of watching violent TV programs report lower aggression tendencies than do children whose parents do not discuss TV violence or restrict access to violent TV shows.[57] Similarly, Nathanson observes that parental co-viewing or commenting on the programs reduces the impacts of watching violent TV programs on a child.[58] This is probably because it reduces the child's perception of TV violence as real, reduces child's identification with performer, and reduces the likelihood that child will rehearse the observed violent script in daydream or play immediately after observation. So, with regard to Bandura's Social Learning theory,[59] parents are urged to watch TV violence with children and offering constructive advice aimed at obstructing all characteristics of media violence role models to be modeled by student children.

55. Centerwall, "Exposure to Television" (1992).
56. Huesmann, et al., "Longitudinal Relations" (2003).
57. Huesmann, &Taylor, "The Role of Media" (2006).
58. Nathanson, "Identifying and Explaining the Relationship between Parental Mediation and Children's Aggression (1999).
59. Bandura, "*Social Foundations of Thought*," (1986).

Conclusion

The findings about the impact of watching violent TV programs to the secondary school children were presented and discussed according to their respective objectives. It has been disclosed that most of the children 90.4 percent watch television at home, at the sitting room, in relation to other places. Secondary school children identified violent TV programs which are movies, music, drama and informational, and it is noted that they spend an average of five-and-quarter hours watching them per day, which is more than 35 hours per week. Moreover, the findings revealed that watching violent TV programs affect secondary school children's academic performance as watching displaces time for school activities, influences children to engage in antisocial behavior at school and home which lead them to be suspended and expulsion out of school and truants. These lowers the student children's academic performance since they decrease children's GPA, efficient and effectiveness in doing class assignments and the educational goal are not achieved. Again, it has been unfolded that the more time spent on watching violent TV programs the poorer GPA is scored. Furthermore, the study revealed that watching such a programs school children replicate some of the antisocial behavior which lead them to use abusive language, engage in love affairs, and engage in drug abuse. Documentary review confirms that secondary school children who watch violent TV programs were either suspended or terminated from school due to their disciplinary problems. Additionally, children also assert that parents address the problem by discouraging them to watch such programs, choosing appropriate programs for them and limiting them to watch the programs. The impact of watching violent TV programs is an anxious problem. That's why; the author invites teachers, owners of television industry, and government of Tanzania to have a joint decision on how to rescue our children from the adverse impact of watching violent TV programs rather than leaving parents alone to deal with the problem.

CHAPTER 5

Concluding Remarks

Introduction

This chapter presents the summary of the study, summary of the major findings, the conclusions reached based on the findings, and recommendations for actions and for further researches on the basis of the findings.

Summary and Major Findings

This study investigated the impact of watching violent TV programs to the secondary school children and how to mitigate the problem. Five specific objectives guided the study:

  i. To examine the students' accessibility to television.
 ii. To ascertain the types of violent TV programs and amount of time students spend on them.
iii. To determine ways through which watching violent TV programs affect academic performance of the secondary school children.
 iv. To find out the impact of watching violent TV programs on the discipline of secondary school children.
  v. To examine the role of parents or guardians in addressing the adverse impact of watching violent TV programs on their school children.

The study was guided by two theories. The first one is Bandura's (1971, 1986) Social Learning Theory. It is explained earlier in chapter one that children learn through observing and modeling the behavior of the social role models. This theory also reveals how secondary school children and other youths learn the behavior of social media models being represented on television and then replicate them later. The second one is Gerbner's (1976) Cultivation Theory. This theory is employed to explain how children come to understand and view the world after watching much violent TV programs. It discloses that secondary school children who watch violent TV programs extensively come to perceive the actual world as unsafe as the television world. This perception leads them to take protective measures when walking alone at night or dangerous places

The study was conducted in Mbeya City Council. Three categories of the respondents participated in the study. A total number of 240 secondary school children of between the ages 12–21+ filled in the questionnaires given to them by the researcher. The researcher also had one-to-one interview with 24 teachers and the FGDs with 36 parents/ guardians of secondary school children.

The study used a mixed methods research approach, that is, a combination of both quantitative and qualitative approaches. Qualitative findings were used to compliment quantitative findings. The explanatory sequential research design, one of the mixed methods research designs was also employed. The methods used to collect data include questionnaire, one-to-one interview, FGDs and documentary review. Moreover, instruments were pilot tested and yielded a reliability index of above 0.7 Cronbach's alpha (α). The overall reliability coefficient was 0.818α whereas internal reliability coefficient was 0.846α. The quantitative data were analyzed by using Statistical Package for Social Science (SPSS) version 20, and the descriptive statistics were calculated to obtain frequencies and percentages for easy interpretation. Qualitative data were analyzed thematically to complement quantitative results.

Concluding Remarks
Summary of the Major Findings

This study revealed five important things.

i. All secondary school children had access to television at different places. Most of the children 217 (90.4 percent) accessed TV at home, 217 (90.4 percent) children watched TV at sitting room, and also few of them accessed TV in bedrooms. This suggests that the study area had many people with mid income and few people with high income.

ii. The violent TV programs included movies 231 (96.2 percent), music 224 (93.4 percent), drama 219 (91.3 percent) and TV informational program 219 (91.3 percent).

iii. Most children 170 (70.8 percent) spend one to three hours on watching violent TV programs on week days. During weekends on Saturday 97 (40.8 percent) of the children spent four to six hours while 82 (34.2 percent) children spent seven to nine hours watching TV. On Sunday 96 (40 percent) of students spent seven to nine hours, and about 50 (20.8 percent) use four to six hours. Thus, during the week days secondary school children spend fewer hours watching TV compared to weekend days.

iv. Watching violent TV programs affected academic performance of the secondary school children through displacement of time 237 (99 percent), practicing antisocial behavior at home and at school 232 (96.7 percent), and truancy 211 (88 percent). In addition, the impact of watching violent TV programs to the secondary school children was noted to decrease the GPA 231 (96 percent), lower children's efficient and effectiveness in doing classroom assignments 228 (95 percent), and poor achievement of educational goals 198 (82.5 percent). Moreover, the documentary review indicated that only 37 (15.4 percent) children out of 240 passed the exam with an E and B+ grade.

v. The impact of watching violent TV programs on the discipline of the children include the use of abusive language 221

(92 percent), engagement in love affairs 214 (89.2 percent), and drug abuse 209 (87.1 percent), as well as arguing and fighting with teachers 89 (37.5 percent).

vi. The role of parents/guardians in addressing the impact of watching violent TV programs on the children who were found watching violent programs were discouraging secondary school children to watch them, choosing appropriate TV programs for their children, and limiting them from watching violent TV programs.

Conclusions

In the light of the findings discussed in this study, the following conclusions are made. The findings on the secondary school children's accessibility to television were examined. Findings revealed that secondary school children access television at different places such as at home, neighbors' households, public halls, showrooms and in bedrooms. Affluence and the people with mid income allow children to watch TV at sitting rooms and in their bedrooms; however, these groups of people comprise a little number of secondary school children. Hence, the findings disclosed that most of the students have TV set at home and watch at the sitting room.

Moreover, the findings on the secondary school children's responses on identifying violent TV programs with acts were also ascertained. Secondary school children identified five violent TV programs such as movies, music, drama, sports and games, and informational programs. The first three were identified as the most violent TV programs. Television movies programs show humiliation, killings, fighting, robbery, and sexual acts; music programs show verbal abuse and sexual harassment acts; and television drama programs represent sexual acts, theft, killings, slaps, shootings, drug abuse, and terrorist, and brutality acts. As a result, parents and/or guardians were less tolerance to let children continue to watch in their presence.

Concluding Remarks

The amount of time secondary school children spent on watching violent TV programs was ascertained. Findings revealed that children watch programs both on week days, that is, Monday to Friday, and on weekends, that is, Saturday and Sunday. It is noted that on week days secondary school children spent an average of three hours watching violent programs whereas on weekends they spent an average of seven-and-half hours. So, children spend an average of five-and-quarter hours watching violent TV programs per day, that is, more than 35 hours per week. This amount of time is more likely to hurt their academic performance; however, the same amount of time spending on watching non-violent TV programs will hurt children's academic performance as well.

The ways through which watching violent TV programs affects secondary school children's academic performance were determined. The results disclosed that watching violent TV programs affects children's academic performance through the displacement of time which means the time for engaging in school activities such as doing class assignments, take home assignments, and group discussions is replaced by watching violent TV programs. Another way is through practicing antisocial behavior at home and school premises. When children watch violent TV programs they identify with violent media role models and they replicate the behavior both at home and school premises as a result they fight with elder brother and peers and become either suspended or expelled out from school. Some students become truants for watching violent TV programs gratification. Therefore, through these ways watching violent TV programs hurts secondary school children's academic performance to the greatest extent.

The impacts of watching violent TV programs on the secondary school children's academic performance were determined. The results unfolded that watching violent TV programs decreases children's grade point average, lowers children's efficient and effectiveness of doing class assignments, and poor achievement of children's educational goals. Documentary review findings also revealed that children who spent four to six and above hours watching violent programs score the poorest grades in academia.

Thus, watching violent TV programs has negative impacts to the secondary school children's academic performance; however, it is also noted that watching non-violent TV programs will have similar impacts when the same amount of time is spent by children. Therefore, there is a negative relationship between the time spent on both watching non- violent and violent TV programs and academic performance of the secondary school children.

The impacts of watching violent TV programs to the secondary school children's discipline were found. The results showed that children imitate and model the disciplinary problems represented on television by their identified role models. The disciplinary problems modeled in their social environment include the use of abusive language, engaging in love affairs and in drug abuse, and stealing others' properties. Documentary review also disclosed that secondary school children who engaged in drug abuse, extreme truancy, were terminated out from school whereas those who were leaving school premises without permission were suspended. Secondary school children who consistently watch violent TV programs observe and imitate aggressive and other antisocial behaviors exhibited by TV role models and reproduce them in the similar situation. As a result, they either become suspended or expelled out from school depending on the decision made by school governing board.

Parents or guardians' roles in addressing the impact of watching violent programs to the secondary school children were examined. Findings revealed that parents' roles were to discourage them to watch violent TV programs, to choose appropriate programs for them, and limiting them to watch violent TV programs. Thus, parent or guardians are in a position to rescue their school going children from deleterious effects caused by watching violent TV programs.

Recommendations for actions and Further Research

This study has revealed the impact of watching violent TV programs to the secondary school children. This study recommends

Concluding Remarks

the means of minimizing the impacts resulting from watching violent TV programs to the parents, teachers, Government of the United Republic of Tanzania and the television industry authorities.

Recommendation for actions

In order to reduce the impacts associated with watching violent TV programs, the following recommendations are made to parents, teachers, government, and to television industry authorities: First, Parents or guardians should not allow children to possess television in their bedrooms. The reason behind is that secondary school children feel free to watch all violent TV programs in their bedrooms. It is also a privacy place where they can watch television violence extensively if not intervened. If children are addicted with watching violent TV programs can decide to watch them at low voice if parents are within home environment. In absence of their parents they become free to watch even at high voice. It is noted earlier that watching violent TV programs extensively hurts both the academic performance and the discipline of the secondary school children to the greatest extent. Therefore, parents or guardians are urged to keep children's bedrooms television free to save their children from those demerits resulting from watching violent TV programs.

The second way of reducing the impacts of watching violent TV programs is that parents/guardians are required to choose TV programs and watch together with children, and telling them what they are fond of and dislike and giving reasons as to why they say yes or no to some TV programs. With this attempt secondary school children and other children come to understand that their parents are selective and want them to watch only non-violent TV programs such as educational, health, and religious programs. In case of watching violent TV programs such as informational, sports and games and others, parents or guardians should thoughtfully have a purpose of educating their children or discussing the advantages and disadvantages of watching such programs and then telling them what they like and do not like and why. As a result, children will also become selective to watching TV programs which are beneficial to their academic and social world.

The third way is that parents should allow their secondary school children to watch high quality and non-violent TV programs for one to two hours per day. The reason behind is that watching high quality non-violent TV programs extensively also have negative relationship with academic performance of the school going children. Children's academic performance is negatively affected by spending much time on watching any type TV programs. For that reason, parents or guardians are advised not to allow their student children to watch appropriate TV programs for more than two hours, however, poor academic performance of some children are a result of individual attribution.

The fourth way of minimizing the impacts of watching violent TV programs to the secondary school children is that parents have to set clear rules regarding children's TV use in their homes and other places. At home, secondary school children and other children should be allowed to watch TV programs only in the presence of their parents. They should watch appropriate TV programs only for an hour in week days and not more than two hours on weekend days which will enable them to have enough time either for school assignments or home chores. In other places, parents should not allow their school going children to watch TV in other places such as neighbors' households, public TV halls and show rooms since they are not sure about the type of TV programs they are going to watch and how much do they watch. Hence, setting rules for permission to watch TV programs, what to watch, how much to watch, and where to watch will help much to minimize the problem only if all parents will adhere to the rules recommended and friendly discussing with them as to why they decided to impose such rules.

The fifth way is that parents should teach their children to ask permission to use TV and other media. Parents should ensure that children understand the teaching precisely and then make a compromise with them that they have to ask permission to watch

Concluding Remarks

appropriate TV programs only. The permission should be offered only when parents are at home and if not elder sisters or brothers who knows why parents have decided so and they adhere to the rules set by parents. As a result, parents will be aware of the content of TV programs their children are consuming and at the same time they will be safe from the influence of violent TV role models.

Teachers also have a great role to play to minimize the impacts of watching violent TV programs to the secondary school children. Teachers are very important figures in our societies worldwide since all the literate people and the international figures have passed through the hands of teachers. They are vividly known to impart knowledge, skills, attitudes and values to their learners. Teachers are urged to provide media education to their learners to be TV literate as a means of protecting them against deleterious health effects of watching violent TV programs. They have to teach secondary school children including other children on how TV works, how TV can influence the ways we perceive truth and build up rational thoughts, and how to disagree with harmful messages. Teachers also have a responsibility to reveal that watching violent TV programs extensively have a negative relationship to both the academic performance and discipline of the secondary school children. Moreover, teachers should be able educate their learners that suitable TV programs if watched lengthily also have the same effect to the academic performance of the children. Then be able to advise their learners to watch educative and suitable TV programs only and that they should not spend more than one hour on the week days and not more than two hour on weekend days. As a result, school children will be performing better in academics and become good citizens and practicing prosocial behavior.

The government also is responsible to minimize the impact of watching violent TV programs to the secondary school children. It is advised to address publicly about the disadvantages of watching violent TV content and then join hand by providing research funding sources to establish media violence including TV violence on the public health agenda. The research funding sources will enable researchers to do their work and bringing research report on how media violence is harming our school going children and then suggesting the means of overcoming the problem. Hence, the public talk about the demerits of watching violent TV programs and the provision of research funds will contribute to the reduction of the problem.

Moreover, the government also should impose a policy that would neither allow an individual nor formal or informal organization to show violence on TV in public halls and showrooms during class hours. This will enable school truants who prefer watching violent TV programs to studies will start to stay at school until the end of class hours. There should also be a working prohibition rule that does not allow under 18 children to watch violent TV programs even after class hours. Therefore, adhering to the policy and rules will contribute to the minimization of the impact of watching violent TV programs to the secondary school children as well as to the primary and pre-primary school children.

Curriculum developers have to establish media violence education in schools in order to let students become acquainted with pros and cons of watching violent TV programs. The Television subject content to be covered by the school going children should include the following:

- Historical background of the television industry
- Television theories
- Differentiating television as a passive medium from interactive media
- Students' accessibility to the television
- Identifying the violent and the non- violent TV programs
- How television influence youngsters to identify with media role models
- Critically examining advantages and disadvantages of the TV programs to their academic performance and discipline.
- What to watch and how much would be beneficial to them as students.

Concluding Remarks

- The application of television programs' knowledge into their lives

This subject content if properly taught by the teachers hopefully school going children will be able to understand how violent TV programs became an enemy of their academic performance and discipline. As a result, school going children who are going to cling to the teachers' teaching will become safe from the deleterious impacts of watching violent TV programs.

The television industry authorities have their contribution to the reduction of the impact of watching violent TV programs to the secondary school children. They are recommended to keep away from the desirability of weapon holding and regularization of violence as the suitable ways of resolution to problems.[1] The logic behind is that weapon possession influences children to use them when the similar situation allows them as if there is no other means of working out with the problems. Hence, television industry authorities adhering to this recommendation will be joining hand the researcher to reduce the effects of watching violent TV programs to the children.

Television industry authorities are also urged to get rid of any kind of violent behavior and bloodshed between interpersonal and intergroup. The reason behind is that when secondary school children and other youngsters watch such kind of violence several times will become desensitized to violence. On one hand children would not sympathize with the victims and on the other hand will be ready to shed blood when they are quarrelling with other people. So, because we want to bring up our children to become good citizens who uphold the peaceful life and resolving conflicts peacefully, television industry authorities should eliminate all kinds of violence being represented in television lest our children replicate such behavior.

---

1. American Academy Pediatrics, "Media violence" (2009).

Recommendations for further research

This study has indicated the impacts of watching violent TV programs to the secondary school children. It is obvious that the findings of this study highlighted the presence of interactive media which also might be hurting students' school performance and discipline. With these bases there is a need for other studies on media. Below are recommendations for further research.

First, this study is more a descriptive survey. There is a need to conduct an experimental and observation studies to determine how Tanzanian secondary school children behave immediately after watching violent TV programs. Experimental and observation studies are very important to examine short-term effect of watching violent TV programs. Hence, this research can provide insight into the impacts of violent TV programs has on violent behavior and how children become influenced directly by their television role models.

The second area for further research is longitudinal studies. These are indeed needed to be conducted in order to determine long-term effect of watching violent TV programs to the secondary school children's discipline and academic performance over different range of time. Such studies are important because childhood watching of violent TV programs predicts young adult violent behavior for children. Longitudinal studies assess the behavior of a child at interval of either three or four and five years depending on the researcher's project plan. The studies helps us to predicts the behavior of a child who watches violent TV programs at the age of six to start behaving violently after some years later, for example, at the age of 18, that is, about 12 years later. Therefore, they precaution us that if the child does not replicate the behavior learned at early stage of his/her age then it will be replicated for some time later, and if the behavior is inappropriate better to stop it immediately.

Third, the study was concerned with impact of non-interactive visual medium, that is, television. Other studies can be done on interactive media, and see how they affect academic performance

Concluding Remarks

and discipline of children in general. The interactive media are the ones which allow the users to interact with them, for example, computer, video games, mobile phones and many others. Studies on violent interactive media are important because we want to know to what extent they hurt children's school performance and discipline as most of the school going children they are fond of using them. That is why, besides passive media there is a need to conduct research studies on interactive media in Tanzania and Africa as a whole. Hopefully, the research findings will enlighten researchers as to what steps to be taken to reduce the impacts to the youngsters and school going children.

Furthermore, this study dealt with the impacts of watching violent TV programs to the secondary school children specifically in Mbeya City, Tanzania. Other studies can be done outside Mbeya region or at national level. These studies are of vital ones because will enable researchers to know how the Tanzanian school going children are affected academically and disciplinarily. As a result, these studies will provide an indisputable generalization purpose.

Bibliography

Almasi, M. "The Effects of Television Viewing on Children's Learning." Master Thesis. Dar es Salaam, Tanzania: University of Dar es Salam, 2010.
American Academy Pediatrics. "Media Violence." *Official Journal of American Academy Pediatrics*, 108 (2001) 1222–1227.
American Academy Pediatrics. "AAP Policy Statement." *Children Adolescents and Television* 107 (2001) 423–426.
American Academy Pediatrics. "Media Violence." *Pediatrics*, 124 (2009) 1495–1503.
Anderson, Craig A., Berkowitz Leonard, Donnerstein Edward, Huesmann, Rowell L., Johnson James L., Linz Daniel., Malamuth Neil M., and Wartellar, Ellen. "The Influence of Media Violence on Youth." *Psychology Science in the Public Interest*, 4 (2003) 81–110.
Babbie, Earl. *The Practice of Social Research*. Ninth Edition. Belmont, CA: Wadsworth, 2001.
Bandura, Albert. *Self-efficacy*. New York, NY: Freeman, 1977.
———. *Psychological Modeling: Conflicting Theories*. Chicago: Aldine-Atherton, 1971.
———. *Social Foundations of Thought and Action: A social Cognitive Theory*. Englewood Cliffs, NJ: Prentice-Hall, 1986.
———. "Social Cognitive Theory of Mass Communication." In *Media effects: Advances in Theory and Research*, edited by J. Bryant and D. Zillman, 121–154. Hillsade, NJ: Lawrence Erlbaum, 2002.
Barlett, C.P., Anderson, Craig A., and Swing, E.L. "Video game effects-confirmed, suspected, and speculative." *A Review of Evidence*, 40 (2009) 377-403.
Baron, R.A., Branscombe, N.R., and Byrne, D. *Social Psychology*. Twelfth Edition. New York, NY: Pearson Education, 2009.
Barr-Anderson, Daheia J., Van den Berg, Patricia; Neumark-Sztainer, Dianne; and Story, Mary. "Characteristic Associated with Older Adolescents Who have Television in their Bedrooms." *Pediatrics* 121(2008) 718–724.
Bartlett, James E., Kotrlik, Joe W., and Higgins, Chadwick C. "Organizational Research: Determining Appropriate Sample Size in Survey Research." *Information Technology, Learning, and Performance Journal* 19 (2001) 43–50.

Bibliography

Best, John W., and Kahn, James V. *Research in Education*. Needham Heights: Allyn and Bacon, 1993.

Berkowitz, Leonard. "Situational Influences on Relations to Observed Violence." *Journal of Social Science* 42 (1986) 9–106.

Borzekowski, Dina L., & Robinson, Thomas N. "The Household Media Environment and Academic Achievement among Students." *Arch Pediatrics Medicine.*, 159 (2005) 607–613.

Braun, Virginia, and Clarke, Victoria. "Using Thematic Analysis in Psychology." *Qualitative Research in Psychology* 3 (2006) 77–101. Online at: http://dx.doi.org/10.1191/1478088706qp063oa.

Bushman, Brad J., and Anderson, Craig A. "Media Violence and the American Public: Scientific Facts versus Media Misinformation." *American Psychologists* 56 (2001) 477–489.

Bushman, Brad J., and Huesmann, L. Rowell. "Effects of Televised Violence on Aggression." In *Handbook of Children and the Media,* edited by D. Singer and J. Singer, 223–254. Thousand Oaks, C.A.: Sage, 2001.

Bushman, Brad J., and Anderson, Craig A. "Comfortably Numb: Desensitizing Effects of Violent Media on Helping Others." *Psychological Science* 20 (2009) 273–277.

Centerwall, Brandon S. "Exposure to Television as a Cause of Violence." In *Public Communication Behaviour,* edited by G. Comstock, 1–58. Orlando, Fla: Academic Press, 1992.

Chanfreau, J., Tanner, E., Callanan, M., Paylor, J., Skipp, A., and Todd, L. *The Out of School Activities: Understanding who does what*. London: Routledge, 2014.

Christians, Clifford G., Rotzoll, Kim B., Fackler, Mark; McKee, Kathy B., and Woods, Robert H. *Media Ethics: Cases and Moral Reasoning*. Seventh Edition. Boston: Pearson, 2005.

Cohen, Louis; Manion, Lawrence; and Marrison, Keith. *Research Methods in Education*. Sixth Edition. London: Routledge, 2007.

Cohen, Jonathan and Weimann, Gabriel. "Cultivation Revisited: Some Genres have Some Effects on Viewers." *Communication Reports* 13(2000) 99–135.

Creswell, John W. *Qualitative Inquiry and Research Design: Choosing among Five Approaches*. Second Edition. Thousand Oaks, London: Sage, 2007.

———. *Educational Research: Planning, conducting, and evaluating quantitative and qualitative research*. Fourth Edition. Boston: Pearson, 2012.

Cummings, H.M.M., and Vandewater, E.A.P. "Relation of Adolescent Video Game Play to Time Spent in other Activities." *Archives of Pediatric and Adolescent Medicine* 161 (2007) 684–689.

Daniyal, Muhammad, and Hassan, Ali. "The Impact of Television Programs and Advertisement on School going Adolescents: A Case Study of Bahawalpur City, Pakistan." *Bulgarian Journal of Science and Education Policy (BJSEP)* 7 (2013) 26–36.

Denscombe, Martyn. *The Good Research Guide for Small Scale Social Research Projects*. Second Edition. Buckingham: Open University Press, 2004.

Bibliography

Dowing, J., Mohammadi, A., and Mohammadi, S.A. *Questioning the Media: A Critical Introduction.* Newbury Park: Sage, 1990.

Dubow, Eric F. and Miller, Laurie S. *Television Violence Viewing and Aggressive behaviour.* In *Tuning into young viewers: Social Science Perspectives on Television,* edited by T.M. Macbeth, 33-67. California: Sage, 1996.

Evmorfopoulou, Kalliopi. "Focus Group Methodology for the Madame Project," 2007. Online at: http://www.shef.ac.uk/~scgisa/Madamenew/deliverable FGEnd1.htm.

Gentile, Douglass A., Saleem Muniba, and Anderson Craig, A. "Public Policy and the Effects of Media Violence on Children." *Social Issues and Policy Review* 1 (2007) 15-61.

Gerbner, George. "Reclaim our Cultural Mythology: Television's Global Marketing Strategy Creates a Damaging and Alienated Window on the World." *Ecology of Justice* 14 (1994) 234-369.

Gerbner, George; Gross, Larry; Signorielli, Nancy; and Morgan, Michael. "Television Violence, Victimization, and Power." *American Behavioural Scientists* 23 (1980) 705-716.

Gerbner, George; Morgan, Michael; and Signorielli, Nancy. *Television Viewing and Fear of Victimization: Specification or Spuriousness.* The Annenberg School of Communication, Texas: University of Pennsylvania, 1979.

Goldstein, Jeffrey. *Why we Watch: The Attractions of Violent Entertainment.* New York: Oxford University Press, 1998.

Graham, Judith. *How Television Viewing Affects Children.* Maine: University of Maine Cooperative Extension, 2006.

Greenberg, Bradley S. "British Children and Televised Violence." *Public Opinion Quarterly* 38 (1975) 531-547.

Griffin, Em. *A First Look at Gerbner's Cultivation Theory.* Eighth Edition. New York: McGraw Hill, 2012.

Groebel, Jo. *The UNESCO Global Study on Media Violence: A Joint Project of UNESCO, the World Organization of the Scout Movement and Utrecht University, Netherlands.* Report presented to the Director General of UNESCO, UNESCO: Paris, 1998.

———. "The UNESCO Global Study on Media Violence: The Major Project of Education in Latin America and the Caribbean," 1999. Paper Presented at Santiago, Chile. Online at: http://unesdoc.Unesco.org/images/0011/001178/117881e.pdf

Gunter, Barrie. *Media Research Methods.* London: Sage, 2000.

Hargrave, A.M. "Bad Language in Television and Video Games-What are the Limits," 2008. Online at: http://www.ofcom.org.uk/....badlang. pdf/

Huesmann, Rowell L. (2007). "The Impact of Electronic Media Violence: Scientific Theory and Research." *Journal of Adolescent,* 41(1998) s6-s13.

Huesmann, Rowell L., and Taylor, Laramie D. (2006). "The Role of Media Violence in Violent Behaviour." *Annual Review Public Health* 27 (2006) 393-415.

Bibliography

Huesmann Rowell, L., Moise-Titus, Jessica; Podolski, Cheryl-Lynn; and Eron, Leonard D. "Longitudinal Relations between Children Exposure to TV Violence and their Aggressive and Violent Behaviour in Young Adult: 1977–1992." *Developmental Psychology* 39 (2003) 201–221.

Huesmann, Rowell L. "Psychological Processes Promoting the Relation between Exposure to Media Violence and Aggressive Behaviour by the Viewer." *Journal of Social Issues* 42 (1986) 125–139.

Hughes, Michael. "The Fruits of Cultivation Analysis: A Re-examination of Some Effects of Television Watching." *American Association for Public Opinion Research*, 44 (1980) 287–302. Online at: http://www.jstor.org/stable/2748103.

International Society for Research on Aggression (ISRA). "Report of the Media Violence Commission." *Aggressive Behaviour*, 38 (2012) 335–341.

Johnson, Jeffrey G., Cohen, Patricia; Kasen, Stephanie; and Brook, Judith S. "Extensive Television Viewing and the Development of Attention and Learning Difficulties during Adolescence." *Archives of Pediatrics and Adolescent Medicine* 161 (2007) 480–486.

Kaiser Family Foundation. *Generation M2: Media in Lives of 8-18 Years Old*. Menlo Park, CA: Pearson, 2010.

King Laura, A. (2011). *The Science of Psychology in Modules*. Second Edition. New York: McGraw Hill, 2011.

———. *The Science of Psychology*. New York, NY: McGraw-Hill, 2008.

Kirkorian, Heather L., Wartella, Ellen A., and Anderson, Daniel R. "Children and Electronic Media." *The Future of Children* 18 (2008) 39–61.

Kombo, D. K., and Tromp, D.L.A. *Proposal and Thesis Writing: An Introduction*. Nairobi: Pauline Publications Africa, 2006.

Kothari, C.R. *Research Methodology: Methods and Techniques*. Second Revised Edition. New Delhi: New Age International, 2012.

Kumar, Ranjit. *Research Methodology: A Step by Step Guide for Beginners*. Second Edition. New Delhi: Dorling Kindersley, 2011.

Ledingham, Jane E., Ledingham, Anne C. and Richardson, John E. "The Effect of Media Violence on Children." *Health Canada, National Clearing House on Family Violence Publication* (2003). Online at: http://www.hcsc.gc.ca.

Longman Dictionary of Contemporary English (LDCE). Fourth Edition. Edinburgh: Pearson Education Limited, 2003.

Lwoga, Edda. T., and Matovelo, Doris S. "An Assessment of the Role of TV Broadcasting in Dissemination of Health Information in Tanzania." *Tanzania Health Research Bulletin* 7 (2005) 98–103.

Masadeh, Mousa A. "Focus Group Discussion: Reviews and Practices." *International Journal of Applied Science and Technology* 2 (2012) 63–68.

McIntyre, J., and Teevan, Jr. *Television and Social Behaviour: Television and Adolescent Aggressiveness*. Washington, D.C: Government Printing Office, 1972.

McMillan, J.H., and Schumacher, S. *Research in Education: Evidence-based Inquiry*. Seventh Edition. Boston: Pearson, 2010.

Bibliography

Messner, Steven F. "Television Violence and Violent Crimes: An Aggregate Analysis." *Society for the Study of Social Problems* 33 (1986) 218–235.
Miller, Katherine. *Communication Theory: Perspectives, Processes, and Contexts.* New York: McGraw-Hill, 2005.
Mncube, Vusi and Harber, Clive. *The Dynamics of Violence in South African Schools: Report.* Mackleneuk, Pretoria: University of South Africa, 2013.
MoEVT. "Educational Law of Tanzania No.25 of 1978 from Circular No. 5 of 2011." Dar es Salaam: Dar es Salaam, 2011.
———. *Basic Education Statistics of Tanzania (BEST).* Dar es Salaam: Dar es Salaam, 2013.
Mogalakwe, Monageng. "The Use of Documentary Research Methods, in Social Research." *African Sociological Review* 10 (2006) 221–230.
Morgan, Roy. "Time Spent with Media in Australia," 2009. Online at: http://www.thintv.com.au/media/tv-insight/html.
Msina, V. "Towards Understanding the Impact of Mass Media on Culture in Tanzania." Master's Thesis. Dar es Salaam, Tanzania: University of Dar es Salaam, 2002.
Myers, David G. *Psychology.* (Tenth Edition.). New York: Worth Publishers, 2013.
———. *Social Psychology.* Tenth Edition. New York: McGraw-Hill, 2010.
Mwakalinga, Mona. "The Political Economy of Cinema (Video Film) in Tanzania." *African Review* 40 (2013) 203–217. Online at: http://www.cass.udsm.ac.tz/japdia/assets/mona.pdf.
Nathanson, Amy I. "Identifying and Explaining the Relationship between Parental Mediation and Children's Aggression." *Communication Research* 26 (1999) 124–143.
Nevins, Tara. "The Effect of Media Violence on Health: A Research Report Written for Physicians for Global Survival (Canada) under Its Studentship Program," (2004). Online at: http://pgs.ca/wp-content/uploads.
Nielsen, W. "Home Accessibility to TV Sets in the United States," (2009). Online at: http://www.nielsen.com/us/insight.
Oketunmbi, Ebony O.O. "Cultivation Theory and Mass Communication Research: A Critical Review." *Integrated Academic Journal of Arts, Social Science and Humanities (IAJASH)* 1 (2014) 9–11.
Omari, Issa M. *Educational Psychology for Teachers.* Second Edition. Dar es Salaam: Oxford University Press, 2011.
Patterson, Charlotte J. *Child Development.* New York, NY: McGraw Hill, 2008.
Patton, Michael Q. *Qualitative Evaluation and Research Methods.* Second Edition. Newbury Park, CA: Sage, 1990.
Potter, James W. *Media Literacy.* Fourth Edition. Los Angeles, CA: Sage, 2008.
Pretorius, Amanda. "Violence in South African Children's Television Programmes." Master's Thesis. Pretoria, South Africa: Tshwane University of Technology, 2006.
Punch, Keith F. (2011). *Introduction to Social Research: Quantitative and Qualitative Approaches.* Second Edition. London: Sage, 2011.

Bibliography

Rawlings, Brittany T. (2011). "Reaching an Agreement: Effects of Television Violence on Youth." Master's Thesis. Gonzaga, South Africa: Gonzaga University, 2011.

Roberts, Donald F., Foehr, Ulla G., and Rideout, Victoria J. *Generation M: Media in the Lives of 8-18 Years Old*. Menlo Park, CA: Henry J. Kaiser Family Found, 2005.

Rodman, George. *Mass Media in a Changing World: History Industry Controversy*. Second Edition. New York: McGraw Hill, 2008.

Shanahan, James. "Television and Authoritarianism: Exploring the Concept Mainstreaming." *Political Communication* 15 (1998) 438–495.

Sima, Rebecca G. "The Challenges in the Provision of Counselling Services in Secondary Schools in Tanzania." *Journal of the School of Education of the University of Dar es Salaam* 29 (2010) 113–132.

Slotsve, Tiffany; Carmen, Alex del; Sarver, Mary; and Villareal–Watkins, Rita J. "Television Violence and Aggression: A Retrospective Study." *Southwest Journal of Criminal Justice* 5 (2008) 22–49.

Spencer, Matthew. "What do Parents Need to Know about Children's Television Viewing: Media Literacy Online Project," 2003. Online at: http://interact.uoregon.edu/MediaLit/mlr/readings/articles/whatparents./html.

Stewart, David W., and Shamdasani, Prem N. *Focus Groups: Theory and Practices*. Newbury Park, CA: Sage, 1990.

Thompson, Franklin T., and Austin, William P. "Television Viewing and Academic Achievement Revisited." *Education* 124 (2003) 194–202.

URT. "Household Budget Survey: National Panel Survey Wave 3, 3012/2013 National Bureau Statistics," (2014). Online at: http://www.nbs.go.tz/...

———. "Tanzania Strategic Cities Project- Mbeya City ESIA." Final report. March 2010. Dar es Salam, Tanzania. Online at: http://www.wds.worldbank.org/...

———. "Tanzania National Website United Republic of Tanzania," (2003b). Online at: http://www.tanzania.go.tz/maelezo/massmedia/tvtanzania.html.

Wilson, Barbara J., Smith, Stacy L., Potter, James W., Kunkel, Dale., Linz, Dale., Colvin, Carolyn M, and Donnerstein, Edward. "Violence in Children's Television Programming: Assessing the Risk." *Journal of Communication*, 52 (2002) 5–35.

www.ingramcontent.com/pod-product-compliance
Lightning Source LLC
Chambersburg PA
CBHW050832160426
43192CB00010B/1993